What's Cooking, Mom?

Narratives about Food and Family

The publisher gratefully acknowledges the the financial assistance of the Government of Canada through the Canada Book Fund.

Canada

Demeter Press
140 Holland Street West
P. O. Box 13022
Bradford, ON L3Z 2Y5
Tel: (905) 775-9089
Email: info@demeterpress.org
Website: www.demeterpress.org

Demeter Press logo based on the sculpture "Demeter" by Maria-Luise Bodirsky <www.keramik-atelier.bodirsky.de>

Front cover artwork: Mindy Stricke and Jane Jones

Printed and Bound in Canada

What's cooking, mom? : narratives about food and family / editors, Tanya M. Cassidy and Florence Pasche Guignard.

Includes bibliographical references.
ISBN 978-1-926452-18-0 (paperback)

　　　　1. Food--Social aspects. 2. Mothers. 3. Motherhood. 4. Nutrition. 5. Families. I. Cassidy, Tanya M., 1963-, author , editor II. Pasche Guignard, Florence, 1981-, author, editor III. Title: What is cooking, mom?.

GT2850.W43 2015　　　　394.1'20852　　　　C2015-908172-6

What's Cooking, Mom?

Narratives about Food and Family

EDITED BY

Tanya M. Cassidy and Florence Pasche Guignard

DEMETER

DEMETER PRESS

Table of Contents

Acknowledgements

THE EDITORS WOULD LIKE TO THANK, first and foremost, all the contributors to this volume for bringing not only scholarly expertise but also precious life experience to the table. We also express our gratitude to Professor Andrea O'Reilly, editor-in-chief at Demeter Press, for her invaluable suggestions, advice, and encouragement. We also wish to thank all of the staff at Demeter whose behind the scenes help has been invaluable.

This project was enabled, directly and less directly, by funding from the Horizon 2020 Marie Skłodowska Curie Fellowship and the Swiss National Science Foundation. It has also benefitted from the generous patronage of the Joseph and Drenda Vijuk foundation.

The editors, on behalf of the contributors, would also like to acknowledge the support provided by all who nurture us, including our mothers, fathers, partners, and children as well as all of the significant others in our lives, creating the dynamic familial support networks without which no intellectual enterprise is possible, or indeed, worthwhile.

Introduction

TANYA M. CASSIDY AND FLORENCE PASCHE GUIGNARD

What's Cooking, Mom? Narratives about Food and Family consists of a series of contributions in the memoir tradition, together with autoethnographic, reflexive, and personal discussions. Our original Demeter Press call for papers on the subject of mothers and food resulted in many fascinating abstracts. Following a difficult selection process, we decided to organize the offerings we received around two volumes that we are publishing with Demeter Press, together with a third volume, which is still under negotiation with another Canadian press. All these volumes are in line with a motherhood studies approach that seeks to present authentic and often silenced maternal voices at the center of the inquiry, and this first volume consciously takes a literary and narrative approach. As shown by the many publications relevant to these topics, quoted by our contributors and referenced in the works cited sections of their own chapter, scholarship on motherhood, on food, or on both topics needs not necessarily be based on personal experience. However, through this volume, we deliberately position mothers as more than just objects of study: we position them as active subjects and reflexive narrators.

Some of our contributors are experts in creative writing, while others are scholars in the humanities, the social sciences, and in health research, thus making participation in this volume a unique occasion for reflecting on personal experiences that nevertheless have a much broader relevance. Some chapters are grounded in theory while others are more emotionally spontaneous and take on a narrative turn to share and reflect on some personal elements of the authors' own lives, not just as researchers but as mothers, as spouses, as consumers, and as (sometimes displaced) participants in specific cultures. Some contributions show that many of these roles cannot be easily distinguished from one another, even as we strive to focus not just on gender or on women but also on motherhood, on mothering, and on mothers who are confronted with the task of feeding (their) children and themselves on a daily basis.

Through this interweaving of autoethnography with personal narratives, we aim at making this volume accessible to non-specialist readers interested in issues related to mothers, family, food, and nutrition. Motherhood studies and food studies scholars will also find several chapters of this volume valuable as well as our other edited collection entitled *Mothers and Food: Negotiating Foodways from Maternal Perspectives* (2016). This second volume features more traditionally research-based contributions, extensively referencing the scholarly literature on this topic. In *What's Cooking, Mom? Narratives about Food and Family*, such references are to be found in the works cited sections of the chapters that follow an autoethnographic approach and, in particular, in those that espouse a more formal academic tone. This first volume is to be understood as rather informal—a comfortable potluck or buffet-style get-together with friends and family, in contrast to a stuffy dinner at a high-end formal restaurant. We invite our readers to pick and choose, depending on their own tastes and expectations, focusing their choice of particular chapters or sections. Reading this book can be done just in the same way one shares such a meal: with flexibility, skipping back and forth, or saving some of the chapters for dessert.

This volume contributes to scholarship on gender and food by re-centring the discussion on maternal perspectives. Drawing from and contributing to motherhood studies, it takes seriously maternal voices and resituates them at the centre of a web of interactions that involves a variety of positions and of actors, including other family members such as fathers, children, and grandparents. In addition, several contributors in this volume discuss other key influences from daycares, schools, government, and health care workers. Some contributions also illustrate how stories of families and food are influenced, now more than ever, by the food industry, especially agribusinesses, which lobby for government legislation regarding food production, marketing, and safety. Food products are often aggressively marketed to mothers-as-consumers, although children themselves may also be targeted. Many of these stories show that mothers are not bound to be consumers, but that they can also be critical of such industries or that, in order to feed themselves or their children, they can rely on alternative networks that do not necessarily place profit at the centre of their values. Finally, some of our contributors also explore their own past or present position of mother-as-(re)producer, if not of foodstuff itself than at least of food traditions that are culturally meaningful for their own families or for larger contexts.

The economic, cultural, and even religious specificities of each context and the particular *foodways* and expectations laid on parents and, more particularly, on mothers are important to consider in any discussion of mothers and food, as we now live in a globalizing world and in an interconnected era. People get information from everywhere, and foodstuffs are imported and often available from all over the world. We get online ideas not only for what to serve but also for how to prepare it, frequently with emotive maternal discussions about the choices—often taken within a range of constrained options—that mothers around the world make every day. Several of the narratives and autoethnographic accounts in this volume add texture and complexity to often simplistic views of individual and, more importantly, maternal responsibility regarding the feeding of families. Through such discussions, this volume also intends to contribute to the burgeoning and highly interdisciplinary field of food studies.

Several of the contributions explore multiple and sometimes interdependent aspects of mothering and feeding, and could have occupied several of the sections of this book, organized around three main themes. The first section, dedicated to positionality, ethics, and meanings, includes five chapters centred around re-flexivity and responsibility. Confronting her sometimes conflicting perspective as an expert dietician, as a feminist scholar, and as a mother, Christin L. Seher "talks back to herself" while she recounts her own difficult experiences of breastfeeding and of feeding her son with sensory challenges. In line with the issue of confronting experts, getting help, and negotiating personal responsibility in cases of difficult feeding, Joyce L. Mandell discusses her experiences of being a mother to a child with celiac disease in a gluten-dominated world. In the following chapter, Sarah N. Gatson, who explores positionality from an intersectional perspective, offers an autoethnographic account of maternal food production. She links her discussion to her academic or pedagogical self and to the transmission of gardening and cooking skills. Lorin Basden Arnold then highlights some of the conflicts that arise when confronting particular ethical diets, "good mothering," and the feeding of loved ones. Along with questions of a mother's own dietary preferences the authors also explore issues of limited maternal authority over the family's food choices and responsibility towards the environment and animals. Tanya M. Cassidy, one of the editors of this volume, and her partner, Conrad Brunström, end this first section with a discussion of the meanings of human donor milk. Discussing these meanings for both premature babies and for their mothers, the authors shape their discussion around personal experiences about such breastmilk. By highlighting these highly medicalized experiences of breastmilk and breastfeeding, the authors' intention is not to treat breastfeeding negatively but rather to demonstrate inventive and inspiring communal means by which challenges can be tackled.

The six chapters of the second section of the book centre around memories of food and expose some of the issues that make feeding the family such an intensive and at times challenging work. The narratives in this section further disrupt the normative and culturally constructed impression of women as perfect nurturing mothers, of food work as essentially or naturally feminine and maternal, and of family meals as necessarily happy times. Key to most of the chapters in this section is a reflexive exploration, sometimes distanced in time, of emotions—especially the heightened anxieties of maternal guilt, fear and shame, topics that several contributors address—from different perspectives. First, Robin Silbergleid writes about feeding and weaning her daughter, and about confronting doctors and experts, another recurring theme in this volume. Writing from the perspective and with the distance of a mother whose children are now grown up, B. Lee Murray tackles maternal regret in her discussion of the intensive labour associated not just with preparing but with *producing* food. Her exploration of farm-work culture shows some of the conflicts that might arise when food is emotionally linked to considerations about time as a (scarce) resource. Similarly, Kari O'Driscoll's narrative exposes how feeding a family can become a full-time job. She describes the time spent, and the labour associated with, preparing and *purchasing* food with care while dealing with health related issues, which enhances a sense of maternal responsibility. Writing from the perspective of a grandmother, Dominique O'Neill recalls how and why her "mother did not cook," and how this affected her later role as a mother and a grandmother. Her perspective conveys the reality that some mothers do not cook and that mothers are not the only ones who cook for and with children. Her narrative shows how preparing and eating meals together can potentially be not only a source of pleasure but also of tension. Erica Cavanagh then explores memories about food, in particular about sweets, as an expression of love, and about the expectations placed on American women as wives and mothers in the twentieth century. She shares some of the lessons that her grandmother, the central figure in her chapter, has taught her. Finally, Grace M. Cho's piece examines how her familial maternal history of immigration from Korea to the U.S. influenced her strong desire for exclusive breast-feeding. In addition to sharing her disappointment at not being able to breastfeed exclusively as she had wished, her contribution also reflects on negotiating cultural difference and thus marks a transition to the following section.

In the six chapters of our last section, entitled "Negotiating Cultural Difference," eight contributors share their perspectives regarding food and feeding in both space and time and especially in relationship to cultural traditions. Emily Weiskopf-Ball first asks which lessons mothers can teach their children through "tradition-al foods" as she emphasizes the passing of family traditions that may not always correspond to dominant—but not always widely followed—norms of "healthy eating" in a given context. Florence Pasche Guignard, one of the editors of this volume, and her husband, Thomas Guignard, discuss their experiences as European newcomers navigating cultural differences at the intersection of parenting and foodways in a multicultural urban centre in Canada. Their intertwined narratives underline how culturally construct-ed ideals of good parenting and healthy foodways concern the mother and the father to different extents. Two complementary and contrasting discussions from mothers regarding Japanese food culture follow. They choose different strategies to navigate among their own preferences, those of their children and other relatives, and several sets of sometimes conflicting expectations placed on mothers. Wendy Jones Nakanishi explains how and to what extent, as a long-time resident in Japan married to a Japanese farmer, she embraces cultural differences. Her discussion reflects her awareness of her particular position as a foreigner and as a working mother in a context where most women are expected to stay home to raise their children and do all the domestic work. She also acknowledges the importance and support of her mother-in-law in such uncommon arrangements. In the next chapter, during her stay in Japan, Meredith Stephens reflects on the impact of her very different choices and experiences on her daughters and her-self, and its lasting effects after their relocation to Australia. Her chapter shows how the notion of "healthy food choices," again, is framed as a maternal responsibility and how notions of health vary across cultures. Although these two mothers lived as foreigners in the same country, their experiences of mothering and feeding children were not the same, despite some common elements. Rosa E. Soto and Sharmila Pixy Ferris offer another cultural comparison in a U.S. context. In this partially autoethnographic piece, they use results from a pilot study to discuss Caribbean food and family traditions, echoing elements raised by other authors earlier in this section. Finally, the issue of migration also underpins the excerpt from Dorothy Abram's stage drama titled *The Cooking Lesson.* Shifting from the purely narrative perspective of the other chapters of this collection, in this excerpt from a longer series of plays, she dramatizes in particular the relation to food traditions and notions of home and family, in which the mother plays a central role, for Bhutanese Nepali Hindu refugees in America.

We close this introduction by recognizing the important caveat that it is difficult to speak about mothers and food without being accused of essentialism, of glorifying women's role as nurturer, and therefore reducing women to this role. In many cultures, feeding within the family is often the domain of women, and in particular mothers, although this may be changing in some countries as the recent edited volume about fathers who cook for their family, entitled *Man with Pan* (Donohue), may indicate. A way for feminist scholars to avoid being drawn into this essentialist trap is to point out how the responsibility of "feeding the family" (DeVault) remains highly gendered but also shaped by cultural variations, as several contributions in this volume demonstrate. Acknowledging that the vast majority of food work for the family is still completed by women, and more specifically by mothers, is not the same as positioning food labour as "natural" processes situated at the intersection of both care work and domestic work. Key to all of these narratives is the recognition that the activity of feeding children and families is a crucial aspect of everyday life and therefore deserves to be celebrated and recognized for its centrality in understanding culture, society, and individuals.

This collection has no intention of proposing a normalizing—or worse, a normative—discourse. Particular diets, foodways, feeding, and the food work done by mothers can be positioned as part of the institution of motherhood or as part of a potentially empowering mothering experience, following Adrienne Rich's distinction. As several contributors show, not all experiences of mothering and feeding are as easy, happy, and perfect as marketing efforts and public health agencies would have us believe. Some chapters take an earnest tone to show how difficult the highly gendered work of feeding the family remains, even for those who are more privileged in terms both of socio-economic status and education. Several of our contributors (Seher, O'Driscoll, O'Neill, and Murray) mention the economic and professional constraints that they or their own mothers endured—or that they stomached—during their own childhood. Others (Gatson, Soto and Ferris) reflect on the specific challenges that mothers who are part of ethnic minorities or in situations of economic migration find themselves entangled in and that are often tied to other socio-economic issues.

These challenges provoke creative responses and ongoing initiatives on the part of mothers that illustrate the improvised nature of global maternal foodways. That this edited collection features no chapter written from the perspective of a mother explicitly self-identifying as coming from or dealing with a low-income situation is not a deliberate choice from our part as co-editors but simply reflects the contents of the proposals generated through our widely circulated call for contributions. This absence also serves as a reminder that low-income mothers are more often than not the object of study rather than subjects in their own right. To be sure, some scholarship relays their voices (as do several chapters of our forthcoming volume *Mothers and Food*) and takes them seriously, but most of the time, low-income mothers are prone to be subjected to moralizing discourses (about breastfeeding, children's health and "healthy nutrition," among others) that this volume precisely tries to avoid.

WORKS CITED

DeVault, Marjorie L. *Feeding the Family: The Social Organization of Caring as Gendered Work*. Chicago: The University of Chicago Press, 1994. Print.

Donohue, John, ed. *Man With a Pan: Culinary Adventures of Fathers Who Cook For their Families*. Chapel Hill: Algonquin Books, 2011. Print.

Rich, Adrienne. *Of Woman Born: Motherhood as Experience and Institution*. New York: Norton, 1976. Print.

I.
Positionality, Ethics, and Reflexivity

1.

Talking Back (to Myself)

CHRISTIN L. SEHER

MY PARTNER AND I MADE THE DECISION to start our family with, we had thought, considerable preparation. When we first began to discuss family plans, we intended to wait until the perfect time. But as I moved through my doctoral studies, and as my husband got deeper in his career, it became painfully obvious that our perfect time would never arrive. In the spring of 2010, I was in the process of changing doctoral programs, and we saw this as my opportunity to reprioritize and make time for a baby.

If having a child sounds like a calculated business transaction or investment decision, that would be a fair assessment. It had to be—I am a mother in the academy (Raddon) navigating, like many professional women, a gendered organization (Acker; Acker "Revisiting Class") where the ideal worker is married to the job and keeps family responsibilities distinctly separate from academic life (Williams). I always knew that I wanted to be a mother, yet I also have always known that motherhood would not be what defines me. In considering family, I have spent hours toiling over the potential effects of a baby on tenure status, career advancement, and career satisfaction in the academy, all the while being encouraged to "lean in" to the opportunities coming my way as I prepare to balance the demands of professionalism and motherhood (Sandberg).

Throughout my pregnancy, I used to joke that in becoming a mother, the only thing I was not scared to death about was feeding my son I thought—as I had been so carefully and intentionally taught to think—that at least in this area I had a leg up. I am a

Registered Dietitian Nutritionist (RDN) by trade, a "food and nutrition expert" (Academy of Nutrition & Dietetics), so feeding my son would not be a problem, not for me. I could rattle off, without missing a beat, the correct positions to facilitate latching for a painless breastfeeding experience, the most creative ways to outsmart a picky eater that would (today) trend on Pinterest, and the best methods for fledgling mothers to feed their wildly defiant children in a loving, authoritative way—the *right* way, according to the feeding style research I did as a graduate student. It didn't matter when I spoke to mothers (and I spoke to dozens through my consulting work) that I didn't have children myself or that I never had the experience of feeding my own child because I was *the expert*—trained in theory, armed with ideas, and ready to fight the so-called obesity epidemic with my carefully crafted educational messages around feeding and good nutrition. After all, I learned that successfully involving the parents (wait, strike that, read: the mothers) in nutrition programing efforts was the most successful way to reach their children.

With my son now approaching his fifth birthday, I can say with absolute authenticity, as well as with the unearned confidence that comes with self-identifying as an expert, that there has not been one meal or snack since his birth where I have not felt like a pretentious hypocrite for the ways in which I participated in the perpetuation of a gendered discourse that exists to tell mothers how best to feed their family.

Feeding my son has been, and continues to be, one of the most challenging things I have ever done. The experience has been a constant struggle even with, and often against, my many years of expert training I received in becoming a RDN. In experiencing this dissonance, I have learned much and grown greatly, resulting in many things I would like to say to my profession, to my younger self, and to the students I train every day to be food and nutrition "experts."

The purpose of this reflexive essay, therefore, is to present, through a retelling of my story as a Registered Dietitian Nutritionist and mother to a young child with feeding and sensory challenges, the contrast (and conflict) between the position of "expert nutrition professional" and "expert mother" when it comes to feeding my family. I aim to use this chapter as space for consciousness-raising to push those in the nutrition and dietetics profession, among others, to consider the unintended consequences of the guidelines that we advocate and messages that we send to mothers about their responsibilities in feeding the family. I aim to illustrate how we, as a profession, position food as an extension of "good motherhood" through our work with the public and illustrate the profound impact this has on women's lived experiences. Ultimately, I intend to use this piece as a way to "talk back"— to disrupt, to challenge, and to bring awareness to the role nutrition professionals play in contributing to gendered notions around feeding the family.

There are many experiences that I could pull from to illustrate the tension among public health policy, nutrition guidance, my professional identity as a RDN, and the lived reality that I have experienced as a mother these last four years. Below I elaborate on and offer three lessons that I have learned through my journey; I present these with the intentionality and reflexivity of a critical feminist scholar, in the hopes of sparking a much-needed dialogue about the ways in which (often well-intentioned) health care professionals construct discourse around the feeding of the family.

LESSON NUMBER ONE:
BREASTFEEDING MAY NOT BE BEST FOR EVERYONE

As a dietitian, I teach my students that "breast is best." As a feminist, I advocate to free women from the sexualized discourse that objectifies bodies. Both roles include changing public perception on breastfeeding, supporting women who choose to breastfeed, creating spaces and places for breastfeeding to be normalized, and educating people on the importance of policy work that supports breastfeeding mothers. There are a host of social, emotional, and health benefits to breastfeeding that warrant, at the least, serious consideration by every mother. But as a mother who failed to successfully breastfeed her child, I can also say that breast may *not* be best for many women.

I know that uttering such a statement will spark a heated debate in the U.S., but my intent is only to point out the importance of remembering that breastfeeding is a choice, at least for many women in America. As much as we advocate for the right to breastfeed and the rights of those who choose to do so, equal effort is spent vilifying (sometimes unintentionally) those women who do not or cannot – which further adds to the guilt and stress felt by new mothers in navigating their role in feeding their children.

My experience with breastfeeding was nothing short of miserable. I delivered my child in a baby-friendly hospital and planned to breastfeed, even though I was apprehensive about it from the start. But I had been taught that it was the best thing to do for my son. And what mother wants to start off her child's life choosing anything less? When my son was born, he had trouble latching from the onset. As a result, I was subjected in my hospital room to a barrage of lactation consultants, pulling my nipples in ways that I had never imaged. I felt more than slightly violated and began to resent that tiny, little being who seemingly refused to respond to the tricks and tips being passed on by the experts. Despite the frustration and pain, I kept with it: through the extra day he spent in the hospital due to jaundice when he was not getting enough protein and fluid from breast milk; through the biliblanket he wore for eight days plugged into the wall until we could supplement enough formula to flush the bilirubin out of his system; and through going back to teaching less than a week after he was born. All the while I watched my son struggle to suckle, saw my milk supply dwindle, and wondered why this was so hard for us. After about eight weeks of pumping and giving him both breast milk and formula, I finally gave up when my husband convinced me that feeding my son in this way was not worth my sanity and well-being. I gave up only when I had the permission of someone else to quit. Some would say that I was never going to be successful at breastfeeding because I truly did not want to do it in the first place, that I didn't try hard enough, didn't attend the support groups at the hospital, didn't find a peer mentor, or that I relied too much on pumping too early on. Others would blame my failure at breastfeeding on my going back to work, on the lack of family-friendly policies in the U.S. for breastfeeding mothers, or on the discourses and cultural influences that built the discomfort that I felt at using my body this publicly and in this way.

The reader might imagine that this part of the story ends here and that I tell this anecdote about my early feeding struggles only as a lesson in how the introduction of formula improved my feeding relationship with my son. But in truth, the decision to formula feed was just one milestone of many on a long road of early feeding troubles that introduced more conflicts between competing identities and caused me to question the notion of expertise itself.

Within the first six months of his life, my son was put on six different formulas, from the most basic to the most elemental (at more than $150 a can). The *dietitian* in me knew that switching formula this often was not a best practice, yet as a *mother* desperate for her son to eat more than two ounces of formula at a time, I listened to the paediatrician who recommended the changes. At three weeks old, my son was diagnosed with acid reflux and over those same six months was put on three different types of medication, some in dosages appropriate for adults. The dietitian in me knew that this was not necessary, yet as a mother desperate for her son to eat without vomiting, I listened. At approximately four weeks, when changes to formula and medication, and a referral to a paediatric gastrointestinal specialist failed to resolve the challenges, my son was diagnosed with a milk allergy. The dietitian in me knew that true milk allergies are highly misdiagnosed in infancy, yet the mother desperate for answers as to why her baby boy cried endlessly for more than eight hours every day *still listened*, which I now realise was because I was caught up in questioning whether these feeding problems were the result of my failure to breastfeed.

Right around the time when my son turned six months old, I finally stopped listening to the (non-nutrition) experts, and I let the dietitian in me take over. I made the unilateral decision to switch to a new formula after doing some research, and I stopped giving him reflux medication and stopped following up with the gastrointestinal specialist. The turnaround was instantaneous, and I vividly remember the day that he started drinking more than three ounces of formula at one time; within a week, he had almost doubled his fluid intake, was interacting more with his environment, and was not crying as much. At that time, I learned what I thought was a valuable lesson about expertise; however, that was not the lesson that I really needed to learn.

LESSON NUMBER TWO:
GETTING YOUR CHILDREN TO EAT THEIR VEGETABLES IS NOT THE ONLY WAY TO DEMONSTRATE THAT YOU ARE A GOOD MOTHER

With the formula feeding problems resolving, I quickly encountered a new problem: transitioning to solid foods. I made my own baby food (as any good dietitian and twenty-first-century supermom would!) and introduced single-ingredient blends of exotic fruits and vegetables so he would experience a variety of flavours (I still question what made me think pureed artichokes was normal). But my son, despite being interested in solid food, always ate such small amounts, *like really small*—a one or two ounce portion per meal for months. The dietitian in me knew that young children can control their appetite and could self-regulate well, so the concerned mother in me listened, even as he was barely plotting on the growth chart. He also often gagged on food as we were feeding him. The dietitian in me evaluated his tongue thrust motion as a sign that he was, indeed, ready for solid foods, while the mother in me assumed the gagging was my fault for giving too much on the spoon; so the mother in me allowed meals to take almost an hour, went at his pace, and felt bad for putting so much food on the spoon that he would gag.

As he continued to grow, however, we kept noticing more problems. The transition from a bottle to a sippy cup went slower than normal, so I bought one of every kind of cup on the market. The introduction of chunky food also proved to be a problem; however, around that time I went from homemade to commercial food (I was a doctoral student, after all, with comprehensive exams to prepare for!), which was a smoother texture than I could make at home, so the problem was solved. And this pattern continued: the comforting rationality of having my own on-site feeding expert who could continuously squelch my feeding concerns, which were heightened by motherly instincts.

The feeding challenges were also forced to the back burner because a host of repeated illnesses required us to think about other things, namely how I could continue to teach, take classes, and complete the duties of my assistantship while my son was constantly ill. From the time he was thirteen months to when he turned twenty-two months, he had nine diagnosed ear infections and a number of upper respiratory tract infections. I still recall the concerned inquiries from a good number of well-intentioned mothers regarding the severity of his cough when we were out and about. I was told by my son's paediatrician that the ear infections were a result of my choosing to put him in daycare. I, of course, immediately and irrationally decided that the lack of antibodies, which he was not receiving through my breast milk, was the cause. That, and a good old-fashioned sense of patriarchy at work that I had little ability to change. As well as feeling guilty for placing him in daycare while he was so young to selfishly advance my academic career, my son's health went untreated as I also was reminded daily of my first, and most fundamental, feeding failure as his mother. Although many women would have been able to move on, I could not, given these continuing health problems and the reality that being in the field of dietetics and my everyday work in public health nutrition reminded me that I had not done what was best for my son.

Yet again, though, it was when I *stopped* listening to these experts, including the expert dietitian in my own head, and started believing the expert mother that I was starting to become that I began to get some answers. After twenty-two months of switching paediatricians, of self-referring to specialists at the local children's hospital, and of receiving many evaluations, I finally learned the real reason that my son had had trouble breastfeeding and eating and had suffered from so many ear infections. He was diagnosed with dysphagia, a problem with swallowing, which required us to thicken all his liquids and to attend speech therapy sessions to retrain him on how to swallow. He was also experiencing hearing loss from the untreated ear infections. When subsequent surgery to place tubes in his ears and remove his adenoids resolved the hearing loss without improving his food intake, we were referred to Occupational Therapy for a feeding evaluation. At therapy, we learned of his sensory processing problems—vestibular, proprioceptive, auditory and tactile—and found more answers to our questions.

Let me pause to describe here a bit of his history with food. For his first three and a half years, my son would not even *touch* a fruit or a vegetable, let alone let it near his lips or eat it. When I would speak to others about this challenge, I would get the sympathetic look that told me that they were going through the same thing with their children, yet I knew this situation was different. When I would bring it up to other professionals, to colleagues or to his paediatrician, I would get the all-too-familiar look that said, "Well, of course you struggle with the healthy stuff. What else are you feeding him?" I was seen as any other mother who lacked the proper knowledge about what to feed my son and was given the same list of tricks to try by people who thought they knew how to feed my son better than I did. But then I would go on to further explain, to those who would actually take the time to listen, that he would not eat ice cream, or candy, or cake, or cookies, either. They would brush off my concerns that his food selectivity was abnormal and would call me lucky for not having to struggle to ration these items in my son's diet.

The mother in me knew something was wrong. Yet I told myself over and over that it was my dietitian expertise clouding my sense of what was normal; I was just being hyper-vigilant about giving him fruits and vegetables. Still, I tried all of the tricks. But he would not touch sauces, dips, or peanut butter; there went covering vegetables in low-calorie ranch dip or getting creative in the kitchen by making ants on a log (celery stuffed with peanut butter, topped with raisins). He did not like breads, applesauce, or yogurt, and he would not even eat macaroni and cheese or spaghetti until he was almost three years old; so there went hiding pureed veggies in the sauce. He loved to cook but refused to eat anything we made, even when we named it something creative that alluded to its super power.

His sensory diagnosis helped explain the food behaviours we were seeing and resulted in a plan of action. I wish that I could say that we are in the clear now after almost two years of occupational therapy, and that he eats like a "normal" child. Although he is improving constantly, our challenge has shifted to grappling with a medical and educational system that does not recognise sensory processing problems independent of other diagnoses, even as we watch our son—developmentally normal in every way—struggle to interact with his world. I remain grateful for my nutrition expertise, for it drove me to purchase ridiculous amounts of freeze dried fruit to attempt to keep his diet varied and to introduce him to new flavours. Yet I am now humbled by it and, most importantly, ferociously challenge this notion of expertise to avoid making others experience how I have felt in navigating my role in feeding my family.

LESSON NUMBER THREE:
NOBODY'S AN EXPERT OVER ANOTHER PERSON

The biggest takeaway for me during this journey, and the one that I hope invites the most discussion, is the notion of expertise itself. Permit me to explain my thinking with a brief metaphor, as it best illustrates what I find problematic in the way health professionals construct our work.

Imagine a professor in comparative literature who has made a career studying the works of one particular poet. Is this person an expert in the work of that artist? I would argue yes: years of formal study have granted that individual a certain expert knowledge about the subject at hand. However, would the professor walk up to the poet and claim to know—better than the poet herself—what she were intending to say when she wrote her poem? Would they challenge the poet's authenticity, experience, or subjectivities? I doubt it. (Perhaps there are a few who would be so bold!) So why is it common practice, and commonly accepted, for those of us in the health professions to do so? Why in the name of objectivity and science is it common for health professionals, myself included, to challenge, to diminish, and to refute the day-to-day experiences of those with whom we work? In my world, we examine "compliance" and "adherence" without the understanding that embodied realities matter a great deal. As the profession of dietetics continues to expand in scope and begins to be questioned through a Critical Dietetics movement, the ways in which we enact our disciplinary knowledge matter, and it warrants further critical examination.

WRAPPING UP WITH WORDS OF CAUTION

There are many reasons why I hesitated to reflect upon my experiences feeding my son in such a public way. In addition to the position of vulnerability such reflection creates both personally and professionally, it is risky to openly question whether the expert status that a profession has crafted is undeserved, unattainable, and potentially harmful to the people with whom we work. Through the retelling of my story, I have tried to voice, in an authentic way, the tensions that exist at the crossroads between professional, disembodied expertise based on objectified knowledge and the often dismissed subjective, embodied experience of being an expert over feeding oneself and one's children.

My biggest fear, however, in sharing my story is that readers will walk away from this essay thinking that my example is unique. I fear that I will somehow have fostered a sense of empathy for my own experience, but that readers may fail to connect what my story illustrates to the scores of mothers who experience similar challenges in feeding their family yet have not found as I have the comfort in knowing that they are rooted in a diagnosable condition. It is easy, as a nutrition professional, to dismiss my experience as being less applicable to the masses because my son's sensory processing differences manifest as a clear set of feeding challenges with a rational explanation. The existence of those clear challenges allow for a plan of action to be created to work through them with the support of occupational and speech therapy.

If you find yourself agreeing with this assessment, I offer these words, in conclusion: be humble in your sense of expertise and do not impose it on others; engage with your patients in ways that value their reality and prioritize empathy over authoritarianism; and most importantly, be open to questioning the ways in which we, as nutrition professionals, construct messages, disproportionately to mothers, around feeding the family.

WORKS CITED

Academy of Nutrition and Dietetics. *Qualifications of a Registered Dietitian Nutritionist*, n.d. Web. 6 March 2015.

Acker, Joan. "Hierarchies, Jobs, Bodies: A Theory of Gendered Organizations." *Gender and Society,* 4.2 (1999): 139-158. Print.

Acker, Joan. "Revisiting class: Thinking from Gender, Race, and

Organizations." *Social Politics: International Studies in Gender, State & Society* 7.2 (2000): 192-214. Print.

Raddon, Arwen. "Mothers in the Academy: Positioned and Positioning within Discourses of the Successful Academic and the Good Mother." *Studies in Higher Education* 27.4 (2002): 387-403. Print.

Sandberg, Sheryl. *Lean In. Women, Work, and the Will to Lead.* New York: Alfred A Knopf, 2013. Print.

Williams, Joan. *Unbending Gender: Why Family and Work Conflict and What To Do About It.* New York - Oxford: Oxford University Press, 1999. Print.

2.
It's a Gluten World Out There

A Celiac Mother's Socialization Story

JOYCE L. MANDELL

I CALLED IT THE "JULIE" TEST. Julie was a girl in my daughter Hava's class. She was very tiny just like my daughter. As long as Julie was as small as my child, well then maybe my child was fine as well. Somewhere in third grade, though, Julie shot up, gained weight, and sprouted overnight, growing out of her short pants and baby-sized dresses. No longer did my daughter pass the test. I had the growing suspicion, the deep knowledge in my bones, that something was not right. I would get up in the night, check my own baby book where my mother had kept meticulous records, and compare my own growth at a particular age with my daughter's. A mother knows in her own heart when something is really wrong with her child. I knew even when the pediatrician tried to placate me. "She is healthy and normal," the pediatrician reiterated again at her nine-year-old checkup when she weighed in at thirty-six pounds. "But her weight?" I continued, pointing out her bones, her protruding stomach, and her constant complaints of headaches. "I can even see her heart beating beneath the skin when she is in the bath," I informed the doctor. "Don't worry," the pediatrician tried to reassure me, "she will make up that weight when she is a teenager." Again, I was alone with my own worries, which continued to keep me up at night. Within a month of this appointment when my daughter's anger outbursts got fierce and scary, I brought my child to a psychologist for help. The psychologist took one look at her and reaffirmed what I had really known all along. "You take her back to the doctor and demand testing. There is something really wrong with her," the psychologist told me. I demanded all tests—tests of stool, blood, urine. Within a week, the pediatrician called back with some shocking blood test results. The following week, we made an urgent visit to a gastroenterologist specialist, followed by a full endoscopy of my daughter's small intestine. The surgeon met me and my husband in the hospital waiting room as we paced the floor. He told us that despite all the biopsies he had performed in his career, he had never seen so much damage to a small intestine. He did not even have to wait to get the results back. He could confirm it right there. Our daughter had celiac disease and had probably not received adequate nutrition for years. And so our journey began.[1]

Every mother can tell her own unique story of how her child initially got diagnosed with celiac disease—an autoimmune disorder where the ingestion of gluten found in wheat, rye, barley, and possibly oats, damages the small intestine leading to malnutrition-related disease. When children are diagnosed with celiac disease, it is often the role of the mother to understand the complexities of the gluten-free diet so that the diet is followed safely at home, school and other public places. There is a steep learning curve on understanding how to follow the restrictive gluten-free diet. However, celiac disease is also a "social" disease as children must learn how to navigate and participate safely in the social aspects of eating with family and peers. Parents,[2] and often particularly mothers, are called on to assist their children with their feelings about social exclusion, teasing, and even bullying. This autoethnographic piece will highlight the socialization process of how I and other mothers successfully transitioned to the role of "celiac mother" and the importance of peer-to-peer social support to navigate the journey.

After diagnosis, the logistics of switching to a strict gluten-free diet are shocking. What does it even entail to live gluten-free in a gluten world? My husband and I sit in a conference room at Children's Hospital in Boston with a group of other parents of newly diagnosed celiac children. We are here for a two-hour workshop with a nutritionist who specializes in diets for celiac children. She hands out a huge booklet outlining what gluten is and the surprising places where it can be found, such as in dairy and meat. Even though oats are not per se gluten, they are often grown in fields where wheat has once been sown. Unless planted in designated fields, oats most likely contain gluten. "Remember," the nutritionist warns, "it only takes one little crumb to make a food unsafe." She points to a small black dot on a piece of white paper to symbolize the crumb of dangerous gluten. I shudder. She teaches us how to read labels and reiterates that labels must be read carefully each time we shop since companies can sometimes change ingredients without warning. She instructs us that gluten can even be found in non-food items such as shampoo, toothpaste, medications, glue, play dough, and other art supplies. "Watch out if you have a dog that eats gluten and then might 'kiss' your child," she warns. "Don't ever bring her into a bakery with all that airborne flour she could ingest." My head is swimming with all the information. "Remember, it only takes a crumb to trigger an autoimmune reaction," the nutritionist keeps repeating.

One of the key decisions a mother and family must make is whether or not to maintain an entirely gluten-free household. Some mothers maintain dual kitchens with separate serving dishes, silverware, pots, toasters and utensils. In this way, non-celiac family members have access to gluten while celiac members have safe routines and set-ups where they can eat. I decided that we would maintain a strict gluten-free home so that Hava could open up any drawer or cabinet and know that in this one corner of the world, everything was safe. In that first month of major adjustment, I purged and gave away all our pots and pans, toaster oven, and utensils. I cleaned every surface until my hands cracked. My friend, Ellen, who had been diagnosed with celiac years before, came over to my house and spent a day with me dividing all the food into safe, non-safe, and questionable. Either I tossed out the questionable items or I took the time to call up the companies to ask questions about the product over the phone.

I used to be a lazy shopper and cook. I used to load up at Trader Joe's with bags of frozen pasta dinners that could be heated up in ten minutes. I used to joke that Trader Joe's was a working mother's best helper. We would often go out for pizza or we would go for noodles at our favourite local Vietnamese restaurant. It was a huge shock adjusting to the time demands that I would now need to shop and to cook from scratch. In that first year, especially in the first couple of months, a food shopping expedition could sometimes take up to two hours. I always brought my cell phone to the store. I had a speed dial to my friend Ellen who could answer questions about products. I also called the company for each product I purchased so that I could ask them about their protocols for testing their products for the presence of gluten, their manufacturing procedures, and if the product had been processed on a line that had ever contained gluten. If they advertised their product as "gluten free," I would ask how they determined that and if their product tested out to twenty parts per million, the gold standard level for what is safe for a celiac. I even wondered about the safety of fruit. If a piece of fruit had a little label affixed to the skin, could the label contain some sort of gluten-containing glue substance that would render the fruit unsafe?

Maybe this kind of product questioning seems extreme, but all celiac mothers devote this kind of attention to determining what is safe to give their celiac children, especially in the first transitional year. I never met a celiac mother who knowingly cheated on this diet. As one celiac mother stated, "Cheating is simply not an option!" Celiac parents who slip up on the diet usually do so because the diet is extremely complicated to understand and difficult to maintain. In my own case, we had to be extra vigilant. Despite strict adherence to the gluten free diet, my daughter's celiac blood markers never normalized. The doctors kept gently asking my daughter if she was somehow cheating. I was questioned about what I was feeding her. The nutritionist asked me to write down every product that went into her mouth or touched her body. She underlined each product in green (safe), red (unsafe) and yellow (questionable). She warned us not to trust any product because even products marked gluten free may not be safe since, at the time, there were no gluten-free labeling laws in effect that rendered labeled products safe enough for a celiac to eat. She advised us to rotate foods so that she would not eat too much of one food that might be contributing to her elevated levels. Again, I would wake up in the middle of the night in a panic and review what had gone into her mouth that day. Was it the ice cream? Could it be those fish sticks that she loves? What the hell am I feeding her? How am I, her mother, continuing to poison her?

"Isn't it a mother's job to feed her child? Isn't it the most basic thing to feed your child so she grows?" my friend, Amy, asks me in tears. Amy is another celiac mother who also can't figure out why her celiac daughter on a strict gluten-free diet is still having painful ulcers. Every couple of months, we talk on the phone for hours giving each other the kind of comfort only found with someone who can understand. This illness is so hard on us, the mothers, because we must feed our children. I remember when my daughter was first born, how I leaked milk for her, dripped for her, and fed her from my own body. I would give her myself. For celiac mothers, the recognition that we were feeding our own children "poison," literally food that had wasted away their bodies sometimes for years, is just too painful and too much a source of guilt and shame to bear.

The first year after diagnosis is a crash course on learning what is safe and healthy to feed a celiac child. However, we also must assist our children to handle the emotional ups and downs of living with a food-related disease. Having a child with a food-related illness that prevents them from fully participating in social activities— parties, baking fun, flour volcano science projects—is a reminder of how food functions as the lifeblood of many social connections. People do not realize the importance of food to friendships and socializing until they can no longer partake in them. I had to be the one to educate the school and the teachers on how to create an inclusive environment for my daughter. Other mothers demand to have legally binding special-needs school plans that spell out the contours of what can happen at school so that their children can be safe. We also have to educate the families of peers who have celiac children over for parties and sleepovers on the details of food preparation and separation, the use of plates and utensils, and the risks of cross-contamination in the kitchen, in the dining room, and even in the bathroom.

In my experience, so many good people make the extra effort to ensure that my daughter can be included in a social event. The Latin teacher who always hosts a Latin banquet at her house for the sixth graders to prepare and eat a huge feast worked with me for one month to make sure all ingredients used for the evening would be safe. She was open to experimenting with gluten-free flours that I provided her. Even though my daughter could still not eat the French bread made in the teacher's pans, she could remain in the room because there was no airborne gluten flour in the air. One mother at school who bought treats for the entire class made sure to buy special, prepackaged certified gluten-free cupcakes just for Hava. Other parents of my daughter's friends have invited her over for sleepovers, and they have ensured that she has had access to a private bathroom and that she has had a clean table surface free of crumbs and paper plates to eat the food that she has brought.

Although most people attempt to include my daughter, other times we experience painful social exclusion. At her Montessori school, Hava had three best friends her age in her class. One of these friends had a party the first year Hava was diagnosed. Even though Hava was very close with the particular girl at school, everyone in her grade in both classes was invited to the party except Hava. When I called the mother to try to understand the puzzling situation, the mother confessed that she was not prepared to handle Hava's food needs. Even though I assured the mother that I could provide safe food and offer her clear and easy instructions to keep Hava healthy, Hava was never invited to this good friend's house during the three years she was in class with this friend. I think the mother simply did not want to be bothered. Even a niece who got married gave us a half-hearted invitation to the rehearsal dinner. She suggested that it would be easier if we met them after the dinner since they could not accommodate my daughter. All a mother can do is swallow the hurt she feels for her daughter and become the rock that her daughter needs. We highlight the beautiful acts of kindness and downplay the social slights. That's what I had to learn to do for her that first challenging year.

There is nothing more important than peer-to-peer networks to handle the bumpy adjustment to living with celiac. That first year, we attended each meeting of the Boston Children's Hospital Celiac Support Group and other celiac conferences and gluten-free taste testings. I joined an active celiac listserv whose members around the globe post questions and give answers to support one another. Hava attended an overnight celiac camp in Rhode Island where, for one week a year, she could do all the activities and eat any of the food that the other kids did. Advertising through the Children's Hospital Celiac Support Group, I organized a small cupcake party at our house for local celiac kids and their families. I baked gluten-free cupcakes, whipped up frosting, bought safe candies, and listed all the ingredients used so that the families showing up would know that their kids were safe. Eight girls and their moms arrived that afternoon. Even though celiac strikes both boys and girls, it just so happens that everyone who came that day lived within fifteen minutes of our house and had girls with the disorder ranging from ages nine to fourteen. I felt like crying when I saw the girls smearing frosting, savouring those cupcakes, and laughing and eating together without a worry.

I organized this event for Hava so that she would meet local friends who understood what it was like to live with celiac. When the girls went outside to play, all the moms who congregated in the kitchen began to share. We told our stories of how our daughters were diagnosed. One mother's daughter had just been diagnosed less than a month before and was still continuously vomiting despite the introduction of the diet. We nodded our heads in agreement when a mother admitted that she hated it when so many people responded to her as if she were a pain or a hysterical mom over-reacting to the dangers of gluten for her child. Another mother told the story of going out for an advertised gluten-free pizza and how she was horrified when she saw the cook dip the same ladle in the tomato sauce that he had used on the gluten pizza. All of eyes grew wide, imagining the implications of this mistake. We had tips on where to dine out locally. A new diner was now serving a gluten-free breakfast, even pancakes. The owner has celiac, has a separate cooktop, and knows to keep everything separated. This restaurant may be a good place to try. Another mother warned us that another celiac child kept on getting sick. The contamination was finally traced to the soap in the soap dispenser at school. We nodded in sisterly support. You could never let your guard down. In my kitchen, while our girls were playing, we talked. We shared. We laughed. And one or two of us cried. We all agreed that this local intimate meeting was a great idea, and another mom agreed to host the next get-together.

I thought that I had organized this local group for Hava, but it turned out that it was I and the other moms who desperately needed this group for our own support. Adjusting to being a celiac mom had taken a huge toll on all of us. Financially, we saw our grocery bills rise as we had to pay the premium costs of specialized gluten-free products. For those of us who had been working mothers when our kids were first diagnosed, we either had to leave demanding careers or had to switch to more flexible, part-time work to accommodate the time needed for medical appointments, hospital visits, and initial shopping and cooking gluten free. It did not make financial sense for my husband to leave work. He had significantly more stable and better-paid employment. I could no longer juggle my promising academic career with the demands of celiac mothering. When the university provost where I worked asked me what I was going to do when I quit, I looked him straight in the face and answered, "Well, I am going to cook!" Leaving work or cutting down our hours further affected our family's financial standing, which was another source of worry.

For many of us moms in the group, the stress of having a sick child had also affected our own physical health. One mother in our group lost twenty pounds in the first three months after her child had been diagnosed. Another mom had her first ever abnormal Pap smear; it was her body's reaction to the constant tension. Yet another mom had to have her gall bladder removed. I like to point out some new wrinkles and gray hairs. I had not had these BC: Before Celiac!

For two years, this local group met for gingerbread decorating parties, barbecues, cooking classes with my friend Ellen and the annual Children's Hospital celiac holiday party. In between our get-togethers, I knew that if I had a question or just needed to vent, I could call one of them. Our celiac daughters became real friends, and we supported one another. We may never have had anything in common otherwise, but only these other celiac moms really understood on a deep level what I struggled with and what kept me up at night. None of my other friends ever really understood like that. When one of the mothers' husbands was diagnosed with colon cancer and friends stepped up to provide support to the family during his treatment, this mother only trusted our group of moms to provide safe, gluten-free meals for her celiac family members.

We also helped each other adjust our dreams for our celiac children. One mother mourned that she could not take her daughter to the North End in Boston for cannoli as her father had done for her. She associated love of and for her father with the cannoli that she ate. Another woman had only two dreams for her daughter: that she could have her First Communion at church and that she could drink beer in college. I too had to let go of my desire to travel the world spontaneously with my child. I had always "tasted" the world with my tongue. I can recall a forty-eight-hour train ride from Delhi to Madras in India when I shared a first-class cabin with a Tamil Hindu family. They shared their food with me, and the mother offered me homemade samosas and puri breads. The son, Raju, a handsome young man about my age, slept in the bunk above mine. He didn't say many words to me, but as the two-day trip progressed, he moved from touching my arm to offering to put morsels of food, maybe a special sweet treat or bread, directly into my mouth, feeding me as a parent feeds a small child or as a lover feeds a lover. I have had exciting and memorable travel adventures with my tongue.

I often dream of the adventures that I wanted to have with my own children. I wanted to go for a month or two with Hava to language school to learn Spanish in Costa Rica. I wanted to organize an interfaith trip of Muslims, Jews, and Christians to experience each other's holy spaces in Israel. I wanted to eat real pad thai in Thailand and seek out Buddhist temples, meditate and pray. I had a bucket list of places I wanted to explore and "taste" with my children.

Dreams can be adjusted. My celiac mother friend will be able to take her daughter to the North End for some gluten-free pasta. Her daughter will associate that trip and the eating of that pasta with her mother's love. My other friend's daughter will be able to tote a six pack of gluten-free beer when she eventually goes to college. This mother was also able to work with the priest so that her daughter could have her First Communion last year. The priest put on clean gloves and placed a gluten-free host on her daughter's tongue. She could be a part of her community and break bread together. Travel is no longer spontaneous for us. Travel entails planning every meal, calling ahead for safe restaurants, and carrying a toaster oven and a small box containing a pot, pan, strainer, and utensils. Hava may not be able to be fed by a handsome stranger on a train ride in India. However, travel, though not easy, is not impossible. She will be able to see, hear, smell, feel, and, yes, even taste the world, so long as it is gluten free! Another celiac mother friend was able to take her children on a two-week visit to Tanzania in Africa. They all survived.

Peer-to-peer support has enabled me to make the transition to competent celiac mother. During that first week when Hava was initially diagnosed, I was so frantic and called up an acquaintance that I knew in my community. Jill had had years of experience of celiac mothering since three out of her five children had not only celiac but also diabetes. "How will I ever do this?" I asked Jill. "You will do it!" Jill reassured me. "You can do it! And you have no choice." The very next day, Jill came to our house unannounced offering us a piece of yummy gluten-free chocolate chip banana bread that she had made the night before. "It's safe," she explained to Hava and Jill hugged me. "It will be okay," she said. When I think back on Jill's kindness, I feel like crying. I now try to pass the gift along, the gift of comfort a veteran celiac mom can give to a newbie. I am almost four years into this celiac mothering path. I have the chance to say to new celiac mothers, "It's not easy living in a gluten world, but it does and will get easier. You adapt. You adjust and you watch your child thrive. Here is some gluten free bread. I made it from scratch. Try it. It is safe. It is good."

ENDNOTES

[1]A research study from the University of Maryland Center for Celiac Research discovered that one out of 133 Americans has celiac disease, once considered a rare disease (Fasano et al.). According to Dr. Daniel Leffler of the Beth Israel Deaconess Medical Center in Boston, Massachusetts, it takes on average six to ten years for a symptomatic person to be diagnosed. Children are not routinely

screened for celiac disease in the United States. Blood tests measuring the antibody response are not seen as reliable in children under five years old. My daughter received two false negative antibody tests even though she clearly had had the symptoms of the disease. A diagnosis is only made after a positive endoscopy of the small intestine.

[2]The adjustment of fathers to the "celiac father" role and the impact/stress on the couple bond when dealing with a child's long term illness goes beyond the scope of this chapter. I was personally blessed to have a supportive husband who played a secondary role in our family's adjustment. Although I befriended many mothers whose work lives and careers were diverted to take on the role of "celiac mother," I only met one father who left employment to play the primary caretaker role for his celiac children. The majority of board members of local celiac support groups, volunteers at celiac events and the ones who show up with celiac kids to these events are mothers. Mothers still predominantly play the primary role in the shopping and production of food in most households. In this way, their central tasks are most affected by the change to the gluten-free diet.

WORKS CITED

Fasano, Alessio, et al. "Prevalence of Celiac Disease in At-risk and Not-at-risk Groups in the United States: A Large Multicenter Study." *Archives of Internal Medicine* 163.3 (Feb. 10, 2003): 286-292. Print.

Leffler, Daniel. "Celiac Disease and Management." *Journal of the American Medical Association (JAMA)* 306.14 (October 12, 2011): 1582-1592. Print.

3.

Revisiting and Reconstructing Maternal Sustenance

An Autoethnographic Account of Academic Motherhood

SARAH N. GATSON

ON THE FIRST DAY OF SPRING 2014, I impatiently await the full sunlight so that I can check the garden, pull up any weeds that sprouted overnight, run the hoses, and look for vegetable seedlings breaking through the dirt. After work, often with my son and husband in tow, I pull more weeds, harvest something fresh for dinner (usually winter greens, lettuce, or broccoli), and as my son puts it, "go on a nature trek." Our nature trek is constrained to less than a quarter of an acre, supporting thriving rosemary, oregano, mint, dill, garlic, parsley, onions, beets, lettuces, turnips, broccoli, and kale; sprouting radishes, okra, squash, beans, corn, amaranth, sage, and cucumbers; and germinating carrots, peppers, nasturtiums, cilantro, and sorghum. Reclaiming space from a broken hot tub and rotting deck, repurposing brick flower boxes, and extending capacity with donated containers, we now have a yard farm producing enough to teach myself how to can and preserve food. With two full-time jobs in academe, why has my household taken on the role of food production? It's not because I'm "homeward bound" (Matchar) but rather because I am community bound. Neither am I "opting out," yet another faux trend extolled by the *New York Times Magazine* (Belkin). For me, this project is simultaneously a return to the familial practices of my early childhood and deep genealogical past, and a purposeful exercise in public sociology that integrates research, teaching, and service.

This essay explores the levels of disconnect between mothers' roles in food projects that range from household food production, sustenance of offspring, and consumption. These projects are simultaneously work *of* and *for* the body that are deeply cultural in terms of meanings, arrangements, and technological materials. Taking an intersectional/black feminist approach (King; Crenshaw; Collins *Black Feminist Thought*), I seek to make explicit the ways in which everyday simultaneity is transformed into culturally distinct roles and statuses that, although housed in the same body, are then pitted against one another across the terrain of public discourse and policy (Phillips and Broderick). How concepts such as *production, reproduction,* and *consumption* are gendered, raced, and classed are key social processes that we must understand as projects (Omi and Winant; DeVault) that are centred on bodily needs and socially situated rights. Expanding on a recent exploration of arrangements and meanings of mothering, race, and class (Gatson), I herein examine my social location as a mothering academic engaged in a community food security and service-learning research project. Taking my cue from DeVault's exploration of the "'womanly' project ... of caring for others ... and connecting our lives" and the "[struggle] with conflicts between my ambitions and my commitments to care and connection" (xi), I discuss my efforts to meld this project and these conflicts as part of a project that simultaneously integrates all the roles in my paid job and centres on my own household's changing production and consumption habits. I am thus both a mother teaching her son and other people's children how to produce and share food, and an academic (an *alma mater*; Gatson "Multiracial Motherhood") teaching students how to question farming, food production and distribution, community formation, and inequality. These two sets of activities resolve DeVault's conflict on a personal level, and herein I raise the question of whether they may do so at a macro-level, for mothers *and* fathers, and for people more generally.

In their influential discussion of the racial formation process, Omi and Winant define a social project as a "historically situated ... [effort] in which human bodies and social structures are represented and organised" (55-56). Writing specifically about the perennially popular topic of the community garden, de Monge argues that the concept itself is rarely analyzed with all of its complex and purposeful social projects in mind:

Without much differentiation or attention to these [cultural, ethnic, gendered, raced and classed] intersecting complexities, the universalising 'community garden' heading can invisibilise key 3 symbolic differences, including the degree to which some gardens can institutionalize themselves; the plural articulations of benefits from aesthetic to cultural, and finally the varied extent to which some become conduits through which communities navigate toward more just and culturally appropriate urban food sheds. (iii-iv; see also Morales)

In contrast, public discourse that centres on prescriptions for mothers is part of a deep, tenacious, and much more explicit social project constituting proper womanhood. This public discourse encompasses such projects as the broad and varied deployment of the nineteenth-century True Womanhood/Domesticity discourse (Bauer) as well as very specific instructions for particular tasks set out as the domain of woman, such as child feeding. That women of colour in the United States could ever "return to domesticity" or "opt out" and sever our public-private intersected lives would be even more of a mythologizing return to the past than is the case for the largely imagined "revolution" that Belkin asserted was soon to be sweeping the nation (Belkin; Graff). *Domestic*, *home*, and *labour* have always meant different things for us, and although our own voices have largely been left out of the hegemonic narratives that long for the good old days, it does not mean we do not have our own stories to tell about what our pasts were, and what they mean to us. My mothering and food project, then, is centred first and foremost on placement in a familial web that I experienced as grounded in the Black community.

ONTOGENY RECAPITULATES PHYLOGENY

In the kitchen. Among my earliest memories are sense memories of being in my Papa and Mama's kitchen in the "big house." In its small kitchen with a large walk-in pantry, I remember holding my Papa's coffee cup, being allowed to taste the heavily creamed and sugared coffee—he often saved the last bit of the cup for me before going off to work at a construction site. I remember my Papa making pancakes. I remember my Mama making fried chicken, pork chops, fried potatoes, all cooked on the same stove that heated straightening irons for my aunts' (and occasionally my own) hair, the smells of food mingling with the smell of UltraSheen, the blue-green leave-in moisturizer central to my memories of hair care rituals performed in the kitchen. Her tea cakes, cakes, pies, cobblers, all mixed in the big stoneware bowl, were her domestic labour for her family since leaving school and marrying prior to entering the eighth grade. I remember fried catfish, and her later teaching me how to bait a hook and catch fish. I absorbed my earliest cooking knowledge as I watched her bake without a recipe. I would later make her a recipe box that she only filled with coupons. I remember eating rabbit—only knowing it was rabbit because my youngest uncle, eleven at the time, leaned over and said, "You know, that's Thumper." I know that I've eaten squirrel, but I don't know where or how my Papa procured them. In summer, lunches were simple: red drink (Miller) and bologna and mustard sandwiches. Mama would send me down to the freezer for frozen Wonder bread to toast. I would see the dusty pickling crocks, from a time when she was not also doing paid labour at the nursing home up the street.

In the yard. From the outside, the "big house," at 3832 E. 59th Street, Kansas City, Missouri, was the biggest house that I knew, with four bedrooms upstairs where some of my nine aunts and uncles slept. It was the largest house on the street—the last vestige of a more prosperous, whiter neighbourhood—and it was the only house with extensive stonework and it was the oldest located east of Troost, the then-and-now major racial dividing line of the city. I remember picking fresh green beans, watermelon, and many other vegetables from the large back yard garden. My Papa planted and worked it, reminiscent of farming back in Farmersville, Louisiana, left in the late 1940s. I remember the containers of mulberries that I picked down the street from my grandparents' house in Kansas City. I remember walking or biking from there with my aunts to Junior's, the candy store with the large pickle barrel, and finding wild sunflowers in the abandoned lots on the way back down the street. Grocery shopping required a car trip, though not a long one.

After the Big House. After moving to Columbia, Missouri, where we lived on and off from '71-'74, as my father entered college there, my parents and I had a garden large enough that I remember the patch of corn that I could walk through and hide in. We didn't have any kind of formal garden at home again until I was in high school, although we had several fruit trees in our yard when I was in elementary school. In lieu of a home garden, what we participated in during the late 1970s and mid–1980s were community gardens. I only remember being at a couple of these, but I recall vividly the greenhouse my social worker mother built at Seton Center. I still have the plans for it, somewhere in one of the boxes of papers collected after her 2005 death. It is there that I recall voluntarily first eating spinach—picking leaves right off the plants—and rediscovering the difference between the muck in cans, gross in real life and pouring out into Popeye's gaping cartoon maw, and fresh food. For my grandparents, local grocery stores disappeared while my father, who learned construction from Papa, went on to confront the emergent food desert by building the only full-service grocery store in the area where he grew up and largely worked for his whole life (something he's continued to do—"Supermarket Will Anchor $27.5M Blue Parkway Towne Center"; Krehmeyer). From farming, undertaking a Great Migration, living in a Black neighbourhood, and growing a *yard farm* to experiencing desegregation, resegregation, food deserts, community gardens, and the reintroduction of grocery stores, my Black family's experience thus recapitulates twentieth-century history.

DEVOLUTION TO RE-GROUNDING

My Own Yard. The big house where my Black family was centered is gone now, torn down, and the elusive dream of one day moving back is not likely without sacrificing a hard-won tenured faculty position. How can I recreate the familial and communal anchor that the place was for so many people?

I had no success keeping plants alive until the herbs that I grew in my apartment windowsills in Chicago during graduate school. Upon moving to Texas for my first (and current) academic job, I graduated my potted herbs from an apartment windowsill to an apartment balcony, and finally started to spread out a bit more with the backyard herbs that I grew in my own first house in Bryan. At the same time, the front lawn died from my neglect of middle class status marker. I owned land but was distanced from it as I struggled through the early years of my job. The small fig and lemon trees were just starting to bear fruit when my then-spouse and I moved in 2005 and spent the next four years hiring out lawn care. We eventually let the ornamental plants that I had no interest in die in the drought and attempted to start an herb garden in our atrium located within the centre of our house, where nothing grew in the shade of the flourishing ficus tree. As our son became a sturdy and adventurous toddler, we bought plants at TAMU's annual Horti-culture Department sale and seeds from the local big box Home Improvement stores. We removed our decaying deck, starting with the ever-broken hot tub area off the master bedroom, surrounded by a brick privacy wall. We used the available dirt that was next to the concrete slab and added purchased soil and DIY compost.

That area plus our two repurposed planter boxes around which the main deck had been built gave us two years of sage, basil, oregano, parsley, a lush rosemary bush, and recurring peppers produced in "poor soil" where we had dumped kitchen scraps directly around the plants. By the spring of 2011, when our son was two and a half, we began what I now call our yard farm in earnest and introduced our son to gardening. We let go the landscaping company and let the last of the original landscaping live or die on its own during the (still ongoing) Texas drought. Three years later, we have four 12 feet x 3 feet raised beds and are reclaiming a lawn of thirsty grass and turning it over to edible ground cover. In my process of relearning food-productive gardening and community building—two processes I was raised in—I have simultaneously reinvigorated the research area that has long grounded me in sociology. My experience en-capsulates a return to roots, a merger of home and work that was not possible for earlier generations of my family.

FROM HOME TO WORK:
THE COMMUNITY NETWORKED GARDEN

My experiences have informed not only my personal focus on

family gardening but also my professional interest in community formation. Since 2003, I have been involved in a collaborative project that seeks to increase undergraduate access to authentic research experiences. This effort has been based in a physiology laboratory in the TAMU Veterinary School, engaged in the production of and access to science, and science education and training. This approach integrates research, teaching, and services—the traditional triumvirate of evaluation for academics. The effort resulted in the Research-Intensive Community (RIC) model (consisting of faculty members, experienced graduate students, and undergraduate students divided into interdisciplinary research teams), which facilitates student participation in authentic research without promoting elite-only access to rare research opportunities. Developed organically in order to leverage resources of a particular faculty laboratory (Nordt et al.), it is a model for authentic research training and production (Desai et al.; Gatson et al.) and is a standardized model for regular course-based authentic research training and production (Gatson and Quick).

Beginning in 2011, I started to apply the RIC model to social science, locating it in a writing-intensive course organized around the production of research papers. While successful in terms of producing authentic projects that could be completed in a semester and in terms of producing team-based work, with no ongoing, large, "laboratory" to support a community of scholars, projects produced were still largely short term and individually based. In 2012, I was figuring out a way to bring a comprehensive and collaborative research agenda into the undergraduate classroom. I was then presented with an opportunity in the form of 1) reviving a course that had not been taught for over a decade and was set to be deleted, and 2) participating in the university's service-learning expansion initiative. This also occurred at the tail end of a two-year process of my family attempting to make a two-body move from Texas back to my hometown of Kansas City, wherein I had to redesign my sociological purpose in life; it was now grounded in the sociology of community, which was the subject of the redesigned course that I set myself to teach.

I was already committed to re-grounding myself in the praxis of food and to searching for ways to implement an autoethnographically-centred participatory action research project focused on food security issues in the Brazos Valley, my own (finally) community. As I entered the classroom in the spring of 2013 to teach about community and guide students in developing projects in which they researched aspects of community, I shared the processes I was going through in designing my research. One student in the course conceived a project exploring time as a resource, and as we discussed his work, I encouraged him to consider the exchange of a variety of resources as they each related to time, particularly food (Avila). In the midst of this course and these discussions, and my own increasing food focus at home and at work, I had also started a Junior Master Gardener club for my son and several friends.[1]

My new agenda has facilitated a relearning and reframing of history—how my racially-bounded communities were first tied to the land and its reproductive capacities and then decoupled from them, making "urban" a euphemism for blackness. Watching Stanley Nelson's *Freedom Summer* in June 2014, I learned of Dick Gregory's "food flight" to Mississippi. Although I'd long known of Gregory's nutrition activism, this was a piece of his story, and of the tactics used against blacks asserting their rights at that juncture, of which I had previously been unaware. In response to black attempts to register to vote, black citizens were often punished by being pushed off land, and, in 1963, the local government in Greenwood, Mississippi also engaged in an act of reprisal directed at the entire black community. What they did was shut down the commodities program. What it was, was government surplus food that was sent to poor rural areas. The county official said, 'Well, no, we're not gonna have that,' which is, essentially, put black people and poor people in a position where they could starve during the winter. And this was an especially bad winter (Nelson).

As Adrian Miller notes, this was hardly a new tactic: in the former Confederacy, post-Reconstruction white power controlled sharecroppers through access to both land and food (30-36). Even in officially un-Reconstructed states where slavery had been prevalent (and where sharecropping did not become the new economic niche of black citizens), controlling now free black members of the community by use of access to land was still an explicit tactic. In Unionist Missouri, the Radical Republican faction did not rely on black votes to ensure its power after the Civil War, but instead relied on disfranchising white rebels (Foner 43). For example, as reported in the Kansas City *Daily Journal of Commerce*, in connection with an 1865 Constitutional Convention debate over whether Blacks could be witnesses in legal proceedings, a lengthy debate over the position and ability of Blacks in general occurred.

Mr. Fletcher, an avowed emancipationist, but who sadly needs the emancipation of himself from some of the grossest errors and prejudices of the old pro-slavery regime, got off some of the usual platitudes about legislating for 'white men,' and all that kind of nonsense. Mr. Gilstrap ... thought the Anglo Saxon race had but little representation on the floor; *the legislation asked for would tend to tie the coloured race more closely to the soil* [emphasis added]; God had made distinctions in the races; the Romans had tried for 800 years and failed to civilize the African; the rural districts would not stand this thing; the Convention had been carried away by the excitement of the hour and was being forced out of its true course.[2]

Growing up in this same state over a hundred years later, I was part of a black family that was tied closely to the soil, but not in the way Gilstrap had envisioned. Growing and producing food not for markets but for family, and for a neighbourhood family at that, was what my grandparents modelled—the testimonies over the years attest in particular to my Mama's place as an *othermother* over and above her own ten children (Collins Shifting the Center"). With only one child that I am committed not to be a "total mother" (Wolf) to, I see my new food security project as academic *othermothering* (Gatson).

ENDNOTES

[1]The Junior Master Gardener program was founded on the Texas A&M University campus in 1999, with a mission of "Growing good kids by igniting a passion for learning, success, and service through a unique gardening education" (http://jmgkids.us/what-is-jmg/).

[2]Kansas City *Journal of Commerce*, January 24, 1865. See also *Journal of the Missouri State Convention. Held at the City of St. Louis, January 6 - April 10, 1865*, St. Louis: Missouri Democrat, 25-26.

WORKS CITED

Avila, José C. "Food Access & Time." Presentation at Southwestern Social Science Association Meeting. San Antonio: 17 April 2014. Paper presentation.

Bauer, Dale M. ed. *Charlotte Perkins Gilman, The Yellow Wallpaper*. Boston - New York: Bedford Books, 1998, 61-344. Print.

Belkin, Lisa. "The Opt-Out Revolution." *New York Times Magazine*. October 26, 2003. Web. 5 May 2014.

Collins, Patricia Hill. *Black Feminist Thought*. New York: Routledge, 2000 (1990). Print.

Collins, Patricia Hill. "Shifting the Center: Race, Class, and Feminist Theorizing about Motherhood." *Mothering: Ideology, Experience, and Agency*. Eds. Evelyn Nakano Glenn, Grace Chang, and Linda Rennie Forcey. New York: Routledge, 2000. 45-66. Print.

Crenshaw, Kimberle. "Demarginalizing the Intersection of Race and Sex: A Black Feminist Critique of Antidiscrimination Doctrine, Feminist Theory, and Antiracist Politics." *University of Chicago Legal Forum*. 140. (1989): 139-167. 1989. Print.

de Monge, Elena L'Annunziata. "Following the Plant: The Political Ecology of A Hmong Community Garden." Master's Thesis, Humboldt State University. 2010. Web. 18 March 2013.

Desai, Ketaki V., Sarah N. Gatson, Thomas Stiles, Glen A. Laine, Randolph H. Stewart, and Christopher M. Quick. "Integrating Research and Education at Research-Intensive Universities with Research-Intensive Communities." *Advances in Physiological Education* 32.2 (2008): 136-141. Print.

DeVault, Marjorie. *Feeding the Family: The Social Organization of Caring as Gendered Work*. Chicago: University of Chicago Press, 1991. Print

Foner, Eric. *Reconstruction: America's Unfinished Revolution, 1863-1877*. New York: Harper & Row, 1988. Print.

Gatson, Sarah N. "Multiracial Motherhood: A Genealogical

Exploration." *Patricia Hill Collins: Reconceiving Motherhood.* Ed. Kaila Adia Story. Bradford, Ontario: Demeter Press, 2014. 11-32. Print.

Gatson Sarah N., Randolph H. Stewart, Glen A. Laine, and Christopher M. Quick. "A Case for Centralizing Undergraduate Summer Research Programs: The DeBakey Research-Intensive Community." *FASEB J.* 633.8 (2009): Print.

Gatson, Sarah N., and Christopher M. Quick. "Converting an Undergraduate Research Program into an Undergraduate Cardio-vascular Physiology Class" Poster presentation at Experimental Biology. Boston Convention & Exposition Center, Boston. 20-24 April 2013.

Graff, E. J. "The Opt-Out Myth." *Columbia Journalism Review* 45.6 (2007): 51-4. Web. 5 May 2014.

Krehmeyer, Chris. "Reflections On a Grocery Store." *Beyond Housing.* 2010. Web. 27 August 2014.

Matchar, Emily. *Homeward Bound: Why Women Are Embracing the New Domesticity.* New York: Simon & Schuster, 2013. Print.

Miller, Adrian. *Soul Food: The Surprising Story of an American Cuisine, One Plate at a Time.* Chapel Hill: University of North Carolina Press, 2013. Print.

Morales, Alfonso. "Growing Food and Justice: Dismantling Racism through Sustainable Food Systems." *Cultivating Food Justice: Race, Class, and Sustainability.* Eds. Alison Hope Alkon & Julian Agyeman. Cambridge – London: The MIT Press, 149-176. 2011. Print.

Nordt, Marlo, Josh Meisner, Ranjeet Dongaonkar, Christopher M. Quick, Sarah N. Gatson, Unmil P. Karadkar, and Richard Furuta. "eBat: A Technology-Enriched Life Sciences Research Community." *Proceedings of the American Society for Information Science & Technology,* 43.1(2006): 1-25. Web. 11 October 2007.

Omi, Michael, and Howard Winant. *Racial Formation in the United States: From the 1960s to the 1990s.* New York - London: Routledge, 1994. Print.

Phillips, Nichola and Anne Broderick. "Has Mumsnet Changed Me? SNS influence on Identity Adaptation and Consumption." *Journal of Marketing Management* 30 (2014): 9-10. Web. 5 July 2014.

"Supermarket will anchor $27.5M Blue Parkway Towne Center." *Kansas City Business Journal*. Web. 27 August 2014.

Wolf, Joan B. *Is Breast Best? Taking on the Breastfeeding Experts and the New High Stakes Motherhood*. New York: New York University Press, 2011. Print.

4.
Meeting Myself for Dinner

Negotiating the Multiplicity of Positionality While Feeding the Family

LORIN BASDEN ARNOLD

"This is meat. We're meat."

And with that, the three-year-old poking a fork gingerly at her baked chicken breast summed things up. With the precision of a child, she got right to the heart of the matter. We are meat. In the innocence of this comment, and many others, my daughter provided an opportunity for me to address the wrongs that I see in meat consumption. But, at the same moment, she presented me with a challenge as a mother and spouse, surrounded by omnivores in a culture where meat consumption is viewed as the healthful choice.

LIVING MOTHERHOOD MEANS EXISTING at the intersection of a constellation of expectations and beliefs. Those differing, and sometimes contradictory, aspects of the self get revealed in a multitude of everyday interactions. As a feminist, a vegan[1], a Buddhist, and a mother, I have found the act of feeding my family to be more complex than it might seem on the surface. Food, like all elements of family life, is negotiated in interaction and involves more of the self than is readily apparent in public images of family mealtime.

A variety of scholars have addressed the impact of family meals on children's emotional and physical health or risk behaviours, with a smaller subset examining them from a more relational perspective (McIntosh et al. 623; Pescud and Pettigrew 3). Fewer authors have addressed the family meal experience from the viewpoint of the mother, primarily related to working mothers' time stress (Beshara, Hutchinson and Wilson 696; Kinser 316).

45

Although mothers bring occupational roles into the home, they also inhabit other social spaces while interacting with family. In this work, I explore my struggles enacting my various positions with relation to family food. I consider how my specific experiences of multiple positionality[2] (Alcoff 113-118) reflect the multifaceted nature of family feeding for mothers. I argue that feeding the family is an important complex, relational interaction that mothers encounter from an intersection of multiple social positions, each with its own standards and expectations, and that this experience requires mothers to negotiate patterns of enactments for family feeding, which then impact their understandings of self.

This chapter employs autoethnography and uses personal narrative. Many scholars argue that by passionately and critically analyzing our own narratives, we can access understandings that we might otherwise never reach (Denzin xvii; Ellis 131-132; Ronai 103, 123). As we create and study the self, we break open the constraints of overdetermined beliefs about life trajectories and experiences. Autoethnography is particularly suited to topics difficult to discuss with study participants because of the sensitive nature of the material, perceived social ramifications, guilt, or shame (Philaretou and Allen 65; Ronai 103). Additionally, it is appropriate in feminist research because through such methodology we reject the public-private dichotomy that positions the individual experience as something different from and less than public processes (Ford and Crabtree 56-57; Foster 59). Thus, this method is suited to investigation of motherhood, a life role that is simultaneously placed on a pedestal and silenced in most domains outside of the home.

"MAKING" DINNER

The responsibilities and expectations felt by mothers at the family dinner table are complex. They represent not only cultural understandings of womanhood and mothering but also those related to ethnicities, political and social stances, religious groupings, and more. To understand the demands of family feeding as only maternal nurturing is an oversimplification.

"There are four containers in the fridge, each is marked with what is in it and has instructions for how to cook it." *These were (more or less) the directions that I gave to my spouse as I left for the birth of my sixth child. Though I would only be away for three dinners, I wanted to be sure that everyone was eating right. I had already prepared and frozen several meals for my first week home, as I knew how busy I would be nursing a new baby and recovering from childbirth. And, I knew that the job of feeding the family was still going to be there.*

In many cultures, food preparation and serving is equated with maternal love and caretaking (Bordo 122-124). As mothers make dinner, they understand themselves to be making family and doing motherhood. Although women in North America report that they spend less time cooking than prior generations, they continue to enact a belief that family meal preparation is their responsibility. In 2010, Ochs et al. found that mothers in the United States participate in 81 percent (weekends) to 91 percent (weekdays) of meal preparation and were exclusively responsible for 60 percent of home-cooked meals (67).

Ignoring implications of this pattern on mother stress, role conflicts with work or extended family roles, and mothers' own eating issues, we celebrate it in our media. Commercials idolize the mother in the kitchen she is often baking and presenting her culinary gifts to her children with expressions of amazement and ecstasy on her face. We learn that mothers are expected to happily and skilfully do all of the cooking for their families.

Even though I have taken primary responsibility for these things, I've wondered why. In some ways, the division of labour in my household is based on skill. Yet, clearly it isn't all about skill. There is a reason that I am a better cook than my spouse. I have had years of practice. The knowledge I have is based on training, and not asking my spouse to cook with frequency just reinforces a belief that he can't, which is both inaccurate and dismissive of him, and becomes a cycle that feeds on itself.

Although some households have fathers who do the primary cooking for the family (Donohue) and many have men who cook sometimes, the preparation of family food is intimately connected to motherhood. The ongoing expectation that mothers, regardless of their desire or the other roles they fulfill, should be responsible for food that sustains and delights seems connected, in part, to the way that we understand motherhood overall. Intensive mothering practices ask mothers to put aside the self in favour of a focus on the child (Arnold 51). Mothers are expected to see the world through the eyes of the child and to respond always from that subject position. The primary obligation of motherhood is to achieve a happy and healthy childhood for the children.

There are expectations regarding not only who should be "in charge" of meal preparation (mom), but also what should be served.

> *I'm often asked, "Where do you get your protein? Are your kids vegan too?" I understand the reason for the question. The model of home-cooked meals that I grew up with, and that continues to dominate my experience, is that of "meat and potatoes." I've been taught that meat is the best source of protein and that large quantities of protein are important for bodies, particularly growing bodies. Although I elected, as an adult, to stop eating meat because of my feelings about animal rights, and a few years later extended that choice to veganism, I am still vividly aware of, and affected by, these cultural understandings. My husband grew up in the same culture. And he likes meat; he is a "committed omnivore." So, although I am a vegan, my children are not (unless they later choose to be) and meals are cooked to accommodate vegan, vegetarian, and omnivore diets.*

In mainstream Western culture, public discourse on dietary choices still privileges meat as an item of nutritional value and a symbol of socio-economic status (Cole 706-707). Although vegetables are understood to offer health benefits, a vegetarian diet is presented as one of nutritional insufficiency and deprivation in discourses ranging from pop culture to scholarly research (Cole 708-711; Cole and Morgan 139; Sneijder and te Molder 626-627).

As a feminist and vegan, I feel cranky, and a little guilty, that this is the world I have accepted and created in my own home. I am annoyed by my own feelings of responsibility for feeding and the ways that I have "bought into" the system by reproducing those standards in my house.

The larger social patterns of a culture are kept afloat by the small acts of support that occur in the most basic moments. Within the family and in other institutions of socialization, we reaffirm the idea that good mothering is characterized by the feeding of loved ones. Humans develop enactments of gender through observation of the world and the social rewards and punishments for certain behaviour, and we often reproduce those patterns without conscious effort. That women do learn these expectations can be seen in the data regarding family meal preparation responsibility. This does not mean that no mothers challenge the expectations, but the reality remains that it may seem far more difficult and threatening to reject the standard than to reproduce it.

(RE)PRESENTING POWER AND HIERARCHY AT THE TABLE

As with all communication, family dinner table interactions are sites of power enactment and negotiation (Paugh and Izquierdo 186). Relational power arises from the interactions of the participants as well as from understandings and beliefs regarding their social roles (Rollins and Bahr 620; Dunbar 238). Food and the behaviours related to production and consumption are no less embedded with power issues than any element of family.

"I am going to stop eating all sugar, caffeine, and fat." These words from a teenager both startle me and make me feel approval. And then I wonder what I am supposed to say next. Is it my job to talk her down from a goal that seems unrealistic and potentially signals a problem, or is it my job to let her work out for herself that such a strict plan won't work?

A significant body of research suggests that the development of eating disorders is often related to control. Adolescents and young adults who feel that they have little control over their lives may use food as a mechanism to gain personal power (Haworth-Heoppner 216; Serpell et al. 183). Thus, it is part of the maternal task to help children to develop their sense of empowerment and choice in a variety of life domains, including those related to food.

At the same time, the maternal role requires mothers to manage children's consumption. Mothers viewed as failing to appropriately control children's eating behaviour are open to social punishment (Maher, Fraser, and Wright 242-243). Children who are overweight are seen as maternal failures, as are children who don't eat an "appropriate" diet (Warin et al. 365-366). Mothers' responsibility is related not only to their child's physical condition, but also to their social outcomes. Children who are overweight or have diets different from others frequently experience stigma, social isolation, and bullying (Olsson et al. 982; Puhl and Latner 559-560, 567). These outcomes are often positioned as maternal faults.

Children must be able to make food choices to develop their autonomy and sense of self-control, but mothers are positioned as the managers of children's diets and bodies. The combination of social expectation presents a conundrum.

> We have raised our children with an omnivore diet, and let them select vegetarianism if they choose. Of course, this positions veganism-vegetarianism as the "other." And it means that, since I'm the one who cooks, I must cook meat. Somewhere in my head is a repetitive voice that says I'm not fulfilling my duty as mother or wife if I don't make them what they want. That voice is in stark contrast to the one that reminds me of my obligations to non-human animals.

To be vegan and/or an animal rights activist presupposes both a constant awareness of how the lives of humans and other animals are interconnected and a careful examination of the impacts of human practices on other lives. There is an assumption that those who take these stances educate others, maintain a household consistent with those viewpoints, and avoid participation in acts counter to those perspectives. Vegans seen as failing to do this are presented harshly in media messages (Cole and Morgan 143-145). However, this perspective largely ignores the reality that individuals who embrace such viewpoints have lives tightly coiled with others.

Issues of power and hierarchy are embedded in the positionalities of mothers in ways both complementary and contradictory. The mothering role asks mothers not only to enact power over children (and their diets), while simultaneously surrendering power to the children, but also to maintain primary responsibility for food procurement and preparation. The feminist goal of troubling oppressive social hierarchies calls upon feminists to reject overdetermined understandings of sex roles that reproduce power disparities and to encourage mothers to raise children who feel socially and politically empowered. The vegan identity calls attention to the welfare and autonomy of animals and the elimination of oppression for other beings; this may or may not correlate with understandings of power relationships in a household where people have made different dietary choices.

Any of these roles may create challenges for an individual attempting to satisfy various, sometimes competing, standards of that role. However, mothers occupy more than one role; thus, there may be conflicting power issues both within and between them.

Although the positionalities and challenges discussed here are unique to my specific set of relationships, all mothers potentially occupy roles that may at times seem consistent with one another in regard to feeding the family but at other times may create significant issues. Mothers in homes where multiple religions are practised may face challenges related to religious prescriptions about food and how those combine with social expectations of child happiness. Mothers who work outside the home may face challenges trying to fulfill both occupational and maternal food roles. Mothers may experience expectations related to ethnicity that must be managed in coordination with general food expectations in Westernized culture. Regardless of the particulars of each unique situation, mothers must negotiate practices for enactment of family food consumption, and this process occurs through interaction at the family level and beyond.

AN EVOLVING RECIPE

The concept of positionality is rooted in the idea that the social context of relationships that forms the basis of our identity is constantly changing. How we understand and enact those concepts of self is a process of selection and negotiation. Although there are cultural or social standards for maternal family feeding, there remains space for negotiating different ways of understanding or practicing those roles. Indeed, because each mother's positionalities will vary based on her relational constellations and her interpretations and responses to those relationships, the practice[3] of family feeding must be negotiated.

> *"Okay, can you try one bite?" "No." "Just one." "I can't. There's tofu in there." "Take a bite." What follows is the sound of retching. It's an important lesson in negotiation for me. Now, we stop after the first request to try a bite. To live my beliefs, it is more important to me that my children make their choices than that they make the same choices I do. It's frustrating, sometimes, because the meal I laboured over goes uneaten. I won't make them something else, but I won't make them eat food they find repulsive, any more than I would expect someone to require that I eat meat.*

As control and power are negotiated in relationships, the ability of any individual to assert power rests on the varying resources that he or she can employ. Maternal control over family feeding is complex due to the degree of child centeredness that we have culturally embraced in combination with the expectation that mothers will be able to ensure that children eat a nutritious and culturally acceptable diet.

The way in which this dynamic occurs in any family is a process of interactional development, and the resulting patterns can evolve in a variety of ways depending on which role responsibilities take precedence. In a family where the happiness of the child is primary, children may get to select the meals and the mother makes what is requested. In a family for whom the maternal responsibility for a nutritious diet is primary, children may be presented with a plate of food and required to eat it. In a family that has placed primacy on creating independence and fostering control but is working against the expectation that food provision is a female activity, dinner preparation may occur individually or on a rotating basis. There are many different possibilities, all predicated on what is negotiated in that family.

About half of our family meals are vegetarian. The meat-containing meals usually have meat on the side. With few exceptions, I won't cook meat that involves extensive handling. This isn't a fully comfortable choice for me because I know I'm just saving myself from some trauma and not saving animals or supporting the rights of those beings. But, it is a pattern we've come to, through a process of negotiation, at and away from the table. I tell my spouse that when the kids leave home, he's on his own for cooking meat. We'll see.

This negotiation of family food practices is a process of selection (and thereby deselection) in which social expectations and selves will be priorities in any situation. Members of the family all participate in this development of enactment standards. The reality of having multiple sets of potentially conflicting desires and expectations is that either the desires and expectations must change, possibly through reframing, or some will be privileged over others at any point in time. A mother in interaction with her family and others may choose to prioritize the happiness of family members over her other group affiliations. That same mother may determine that enacting her other roles is important enough that sacrificing some happiness is acceptable.

Although mothers develop particular patterns of negotiated practices of family feeding, it is important to note that these are not fixed, nor do they necessarily alleviate the challenges of multiple roles. Over time, maternal understandings of self will shift as families, cultures, and relationships change. Through these processes, various relationships may become more or less salient to understandings of self and thus change in relative importance to family feeding. Additionally, as families develop particular enactments of feeding expectations, those behaviors affect understandings of self in an iterative process of adjustment. A mother may find herself letting go of a particular expectation at one time, but she may still experience ongoing negative assessment of self because of that choice. Such negative self-evaluation may then result in changes to the family enactment or changes to understandings of self.

The issue of multiple positionalities in operation with regard to the family feeding dynamic is not one we can "fix" as it is simply a part of our complex nature as humans with a multiplicity of relationships and socio-cultural expectations. However, as scholars examining the experiences of mothers, we should seek not to oversimplify the web of roles that are in play in the everyday process of feeding the family. Although maternal responsibility for family food is a taken-for-granted cultural assumption little critiqued in larger social messages, it is crucial that we recognize the ongoing negotiation activities and how it affects understandings of self that occur in the fulfillment of this maternal expectation.

ENDOTES

[1] For a discussion of veganism as a social identity, see Sneijder and te Molder 622-623.

[2] Alcoff argues that we can understand and define the identity of a "woman" in terms of her cultural position within a set of shifting larger contexts and her active interpretations and selections with regard to understanding of self in that position. Here, I use the same concept with regard to other social categories of being.

[3] In using the term "practice," I refer to multiple understandings of behaviour. These include the idea of practice espoused by Bourdieu wherein practice represents everyday behaviours that reflect and reproduce the social forms of domination; the understanding of practice present in Buddhist and yogic thought, such that practice is seen as the application of beliefs and principles to everyday behaviour (Snelling 42); and the common understanding of practice as the means by which we improve or perfect our enactments of behavioural expectations.

WORKS CITED

Alcoff, Linda. "Cultural Feminism Versus Post-Structuralism: The Identity Crisis in Feminist Theory." *Culture/Power/History: A Reader in Contemporary Social Theory*. Eds. Nicholas B Dirks, Geoff Eley, and Sherry B. Ortner. Princeton: Princeton University Press, 1994. 96-122. Print.

Arnold, Lorin Basden. "I Don't Know Where I End and You Begin: Challenging Boundaries of Self and Intensive Mothering." *Intensive Mothering: The Cultural Contradictions of Modern Motherhood*. Ed. Linda Ellis. Bradford, Ontario: Demeter Press, 2015. 47-65. Print.

Beshara, Monica, Amanda Hutchinson, and Carlene Wilson, C. "Preparing Meals Under Time Stress. The Experience of Working Mothers." *Appetite* 55.3 (2010): 695-700. Print.

Bordo, Susan. *Unbearable Weight: Feminism, Western Culture, and the Body*. Berkeley: University of California Press, 1993. Print.

Bourdieu, Pierre. *Outline of a Theory of Practice*. Cambridge: Cambridge University Press, 1977. Print.

Cole, Matthew. "Asceticism and Hedonism in Research Discourses of Veg*anism." *British Food Journal* 110.7 (2008): 706-716. Print.

Cole, Matthew, and Karen Morgan, K. "Vegaphobia: Derogatory Discourses of Veganism and the Reproduction of Speciesism in UK National Newspapers." *The British Journal of Sociology* 62.1 (2011): 134-153. Print.

Denzin, Norman. K. *Interpretive Ethnography: Ethnographic Practices for the 21st Century*. Thousand Oaks, CA: Sage, 1997. Print.

Donohue, John, ed. *Man with a Pan*. Chapel Hill, NC: Algonquin Books, 2011. Print.

Dunbar, Norah E. "Dyadic Power Theory: Constructing a Communication-Based Theory of Relational Power." *Journal of Family Communication* 4.3/4 (2004): 235-248. Print.

Ellis, Carolyn. "Evocative Authoethnography: Writing Emotionally About Our Lives." *Representation and the Text: Re-framing the Narrative Voice*. Eds. William G. Tierney and Yvonna S. Lincoln. Albany, NY: State University of New York Press, 1997. 115-139. Print.

Ford, Leigh Arden, and Robbin D. Crabtree. "Telling, Re-Telling, and Talking About Telling: Disclosure and/as Surviving Incest." *Women's Studies in Communication* 25.2 (2002): 53-87. Print.

Foster, Elissa. "Desiring Dialectical Discourse: A Feminist Ponders the Transition to Motherhood." *Women's Studies in Communication,* 28.1 (2005): 57-83. Print.

Haworth-Hoeppner, Susan. "The Critical Shapes of Body Image: The Role of Culture and Family in the Production of Eating Disorders." *Journal of Marriage and the Family* 62 (2000): 212-227. Print.

Kinser, Amber. "At the Core of the Work/Life Balance Myth: Motherhood and Family Diners." *What Do Mothers Need?: Motherhood Activists and Scholars Speak Out on Maternal Empowerment for the 21st Century.* Ed. Andrea O'Reilly. Bradford, Ontario: Demeter Press, 2012. 316-330. Print.

Maher, JaneMaree, Suzanne Fraser, and Jan Wright. "Framing the Mother: Childhood Obesity, Maternal Responsibility and Care." *Journal of Gender Studies* 19.3 (2010): 233-247. Print.

Ochs, Elinor, Merav Shohet, Belinda Campos, and Margaret Beck. "Coming Together at Dinner: A Study of Working Families. *Workplace Flexibility: Realigning 20th-Century Jobs for a 21st-Century Workforce.* Eds. Kathleen Cjrostemsem and Barbara Schneider. Ithaca: Cornell University Press, 2010. 57-70. Print.

Olsson, Cecilia, Phil Lyon, Agneta Hornell, Anneli Ivarsson, and Yiva Mattson Sydner. "Food that Makes You Different: The Stigma Experienced by Adolescents with Coeliac Disease." *Qualitative Health Research* 19.7 (2009): 976-984. Print.

Paugh, Amy, and Carolina Izquierdo. "Why is this a Battle Every Night? Negotiating Food and Eating in American Dinnertime Interaction." *Journal of Linguistic Anthropology* 19.2 (2009): 185-204. Print.

Pescud, Melanie, and Simone Pettigrew. "Children's Family Dinner Experiences and Attitudes." *Journal of Research for Consumers* 18 (2010): 1-6. Print.

Philaretou, Andreas G. and Allen, Katherine R. "Researching Sensitive Topics through Autoethnographic Means." *The Journal of Men's Studies* 14.1 (2006): 65-78. Print.

Puhl, Rebecca M. and Janet D. Latner. "Stigma, Obesity, and the

Health of the Nation's Children." *Psychological Bulletin* 133.4 (2007): 557-580. Print.

Rollins, Boyd C. and Stephen Bahr. "A Theory of Power Relationships in Marriage." *Journal of Marriage and the Family* 38.4 (1976): 619-627. Print.

Ronai, Carol Rambo. "The Reflexive through Narrative." In *Investigating Subjectivity: Research on Lived Experience*. Eds. Carolyn Ellis and Michael G. Flaherty. Newbury Park: Sage, 1992. 102-124. Print.

Serpell, Lucy, Janet Treasure, John Teasdale, and Victoria Sullivan. "Anorexia Nervosa: Friend or Foe?" *International Journal of Eating Disorders* 25.2 (1999): 177-186. Print.

Snelling, John. *The Buddhist Handbook: A Complete Guide to Buddhist Schools, Teaching, Practice, and History*. Rochester: Inner Traditions, 1999. Print.

Sneijder, Petra, and Hedwig te Molder. "Normalizing Ideological Food Choice and Eating Practices: Identity Work in Online Discussions on Veganism." *Appetite* 52.3 (2009): 621-630. Print.

Warin, Megan, Tanya Zivkovic, Vivienne Moore, and Michael Davies. "Mothers as Smoking Guns: Fetal Overnutrition and the Reproduction of Obesity." *Feminist Psychology* 22.3 (2012): 360-375. Print.

5.
Production, Process, and Parenting

Meanings of Human Milk Donation

TANYA M. CASSIDY AND CONRAD BRUNSTRÖM

MATERNAL MILKMAN

Prowling, precious hours in advance,
No predator more primed than I,
No player in the park more agile,
I spin in search of new arrivals.

From the island's slowest edges and its
Least saleable crenellations
Creep in the endless buses and secreted
Within just one waits
A box

Brimful of pasteurised happiness
Squeezed from a
Plenitude of bosoms.
Frozen, tested, bottled and shared,
Polystyrene cuddles the very milk
Of human very kindness.

So when the one true bus is peeled
I'm there with a smile and a cup and a spoon.
And I'll carry this milk across illiberal pelican crossings
And stand easy with it on trains.
I'll hoist this mighty carton past every glance and snigger.
I won't be coming home empty handed.

Surrounded by mute interrogation
I press play a mute response:
"I could give you twenty guesses...
I could give you a hundred."
So many pumps and pipes, benign pulsations.
Trickledown economics, honed
For the tiny guts and bowels of babyback home.

Born too soon and bred in a box.
Home too late and frantic for pap.
Ingrate? Not yet, just "ungrate" happily
Draining the depot and the donors
And the drips and the ducts.

Oddly bereft of reference is this box, I
Can think of nothing that it's worth its weight in.
The box is life and I'm heaving it.

Box O box O focus all the mamma love with science.
So many mothers in a little room. Meditate (please)
Upon such maternal concentrate. Meantime
Pour it all into the boy.

The boy in this poem is our son, Gabriel, who was born ten weeks prematurely on February 15, 2006, and the box is full of donor human milk for home consumption, something that was only possible because the milk had come from the community based "bank" located in Northern Ireland, but which served (and continues to serve) the island of Ireland as a whole. This bank forms a small part of the global expansion of donor human milk banking (Cassidy) and is the only community bank in the UK. The bank is also a member of the UK Association of Milk Banking (UKAMB; ukamb.org) and a key part of the more recently organized European Milk Banking Association (EMBA; europeanmilkbanking. org). UKAMB is also a co-founding organization, with the Human Milk Banking Association of North America (HMBANA; hmbana. org), of the International Milk Banking Initiative (internationalmilkbanking.org), although Brazil continues to be the global leader in terms of this intervention, funding the largest number of milk banks and spearheading the annual World Day of Human Milk Donation (May 19).

Born to a medical social scientist[1] and an eighteenth-century literary expert on poetry and rhetoric, our son was seemingly destined to receive cutting-edge medical care and to be reimagined in terms of narrative. Gillian Weaver—the director of the oldest donor human milk bank in the UK, and possibly, the world, a former president of UKAMB, and at the time of writing this narrative the president of the EMBA—told us that she often informed mothers and fathers that mothers produced the milk for the infants, but with the need to use breast pumps for many premature infants, fathers were key to the processing of the infant's milk. Commercials for formula milk have attempted to suggest that formula bottle feeding provides a way for fathers to be "more involved" in parenting. The reality is, of course, that being a supportive partner to a breast-feeding mother offers a great many opportunities for practical hands-on involvement, especially for women dependent in some way on breast-pumps (Cassidy, "PumpMoms").

Recently Penny Van Esterik has argued that breastfeeding in general should be considered in terms of both process and product—a material and a relational fusion. These familial links between product and process are the heart of our narrative about family and feeding our son. We offer therefore a prose account of the paternal accounts of the process of infant feeding, and how such accounts intertwine with multi-maternal features of milk as product.

The poem begins at Bus Aras, the bus station in the centre of Dublin, after our son has been released from hospital, and we are unusually fortunate to be able to continue to receive donor human milk at home. Conrad arrives by train because there is not the faintest chance of parking anywhere near this place. He is pacing nervously because the buses are arriving from several different directions. Of course, there is a big electronic board noting arrivals, but he does not trust it because the only thing he trusts is one particular bus and the thing that is inside it. Because, you see, he is not here to go anywhere. He is here to pick something up. And he is here, perhaps an hour in advance, perhaps even longer, since the possibility of missing this particular bus and the thing that is inside is just too terrible to contemplate.

The bus he is looking for comes from Donegal Town. When it finally arrives, with painful slowness, and as part of a queue of identical-looking buses, Conrad leaps into action. He is not interested in the passengers but in the belly of the beast. The driver gets out and hauls open the several doors, and all he can see is suitcases. What Conrad is looking for is behind the suitcases, nuzzling against the very guts of the machine. When he does spot his very heart's desire, pretty much all the passengers have picked up their belongings and gone. It is a long way to and from Donegal Town on some of the Irish roads involved and the driver is anxious to get back home. Meanwhile, he accepts Conrad's strange story that he is indeed entitled to the awkward looking thing in his bus's belly. With the help of a pole with a hook, the driver secures the item and drags it out and into Conrad's extended and very relieved arms.

Now for a walk. The box Conrad's been waiting for is not excessively heavy, comprised mainly of polystyrene, but it is very wide. This box is the entire world to him and there's nothing he'd exchange for it. Its weight is, meanwhile, compounded by a strain in his arms as he reaches to secure its corners. And of course, it is raining as likely as not, and Conrad can move about forty yards at a time before seeking a rest. And he is heading for Connolly Station—almost adjacent to him, only a skip and a jump away for anyone not carrying a giant polystyrene box but a surprising distance away for anyone who is. And there are steps up. The platforms appear so high above street level that the very stairs of Cirith Ungol seem less threatening than the steps that await him and his box.

Before long, however, Conrad is actually on the train with his box. Sometimes the train is empty-ish and he can sit with his box, one hand protectively draped over it, and sometimes it is full-ish, in which case he stands next to his box. A few resentful passengers grumble at how much precious floor space his dear box is taking up. And all the passengers are asking themselves (but never Conrad) the painfully obvious question: "what's in the box?"

And he looks back at them, repeating in his head the response to their collective mute inquiry: "I could give you twenty guesses. I could give you a hundred guesses...."

OTHER PEOPLE'S BREASTMILK

After Gabriel's emergency birth, and while Tanya was still unconscious, Conrad arranged with the neonatologist, Dr. Eugene Dempsey (Dempsey and Miletin), to place an order for donor human milk from The Milk Bank, as it is now named in Irvinestown, Northern Ireland, and it was delivered directly to the hospital the next day.

When Tanya regained consciousness, knowing that colostrum was invaluable for the health of infants in general but especially for babies born too soon, she immediately began to try to express whatever milk she was able to produce. Conrad had obtained a hospital grade pump, which was available for her to use from our son's first day of life. We were both acutely aware that a mother's own milk is a living organism and is designed specifically for her own infant. In fact, studies have shown that human milk changes to reflect the needs of the infant, and for infants born prematurely, the milk has particular components that can improve medical outcomes in terms of both morbidity and mortality, as increasing evidence including the work conducted by Wagner and colleagues shows. In other words, this food can help to reduce or aid in recovery of potential life-threatening infections, specifically Necrotizing Enterocolitis (NEC), one of the leading causes of death among the prematurely born.

We know of this all too personally as our first son, Liam, had been born a year earlier, also ten weeks prematurely, but in Canada, where a decision to feed him artificial formula was taken because the nearest donor human milk bank at the time was over two thousand kilometres away. At sixteen days of age he was diagnosed with NEC and rushed to the nearest level three neonatal surgical unit where doctors quickly determined that there was not enough bowel left to be compatible with life. He died in our arms a few hours later.[2]

When we were able to start to think clearly again, Tanya researched this horrendous disease that had killed our son and discovered that it was one of the leading causes of death among the prematurely born. She also discovered that the disease has much poorer outcomes (including higher rates of death) for infants who had not received an exclusive human milk diet. Tanya wondered what mothers who could not make enough milk, like herself, were meant to do and asked if these infants were doomed to be statistically disadvantaged. As part of this research, Tanya learned that for over a hundred years the answer to the question of how to improve outcomes for prematurely born infants had been medicalized milk exchange, currently understood as donor human milk banking. So it was in 2005 that we discovered that there was only one bank in Canada, located in British Columbia. It would never have been able to help our first son. We also found that there was only one bank on the island of Ireland and that this bank was a wonderful example of cross-border health exchange: it not only took donations from the island as a whole but also supplied milk to any infants whose physician requested it, regardless of which side of the border they were located (Cassidy, "Ireland, Irish Women and Lactation Surrogacy"). Tanya began to design a research project to look at the social and cultural considerations about this health related exchange when we pleasantly discovered that we were expecting another child.

We also discovered that Tanya was statistically more likely to have another premature infant according to research evidence widely published including work in the *British Medical Journal* ("Clinical Evidence"). We prepared ourselves and chose to have our second child in Ireland, where we were assured by our physician and our chosen hospital staff in Dublin that, if necessary, they would obtain donor milk to be used for our second infant.

OUR WORST FEARS AND OUR GREATEST DREAM INTO ONE

Tanya had been in the hospital for over a month suffering from placenta praevia, which caused her heavy vaginal bleeding throughout her second pregnancy. We were later to discover that this condition was related to Tanya's previous pregnancy, but our main concern at that time was to ensure the best possible outcomes both for her and for our second child. Following another episode, in the early morning hours of Conrad's birthday, we were told that Tanya needed to be admitted to a Dublin hospital for the remainder of her pregnancy for her own and the baby's safety. (As Conrad describes it, we experienced a panic stricken late-night high-speed drive to the hospital, arriving in the nick of time with only five weeks to spare.) Unable to move very far, Tanya spent the next month in the hospital when, at thirty weeks' gestation, she began to bleed out again. This time it was so severe that our child was also losing blood, and a decision was made to do an emergency caesarean to save the lives of both mother and child.

Gabriel Louis Cassidy Brunström, unlike his brother, was born in an Irish level three hospital, and from the beginning his feeding was acutely monitored due to the recognized family history associated with NEC. In addition, while Tanya was still unconscious from the surgery, Conrad discussed with their son's neonatologist about placing an order for donor human milk from Northern Ireland. At the same time, Conrad also rented a hospital grade pump for Tanya, a point we had both discussed previously, in order to optimize her lactation success.

After Tanya was cleared to visit Gabriel in the neonatal unit (clearance was granted only after she had achieved the slow and arduous process of eating a single piece of toast), she then began using a pump to produce as much milk as possible. As a result, for the first three days Gabriel exclusively received his mother's own milk. However, Tanya had lost so much blood that she was not producing much milk as she was suffering from what would later be diagnosed as Sheehan's syndrome, a condition linked to excessive bleeding during childbirth, which results in insufficient milk supply (Thompson et al.). Tanya's circumstances highlight the bitter reality that the infants most in need of maternal milk may be the least likely to receive it. Nevertheless, Tanya continued to express approximately eight times a day for Gabriel, but by day four he needed to be supplemented with donor human milk.

For the first month of his life, Gabriel received both his mother's own milk and donor human milk via enteral feeding tubes. While heathy full-term babies demonstrate the ability to coordinate the skills of breathing, sucking, and swallowing, pre-term infants cannot master these skills until approximately thirty-two weeks gestation. Therefore, for the first three or so weeks after birth, Gabriel was not encouraged to master these skills. Although we regularly practised skin-to-skin nurturance with him, we also encouraged him to have non-nutrient suckling (Moore et. al). The hospital neonatal staff informed us that to be able to take him home we needed to decide if he was going to be exclusively breastfed or bottle fed as well. We were also told by staff that if we chose the latter we could take Gabriel home quicker. After discussing the pros and cons of this issue with Tanya's sister, a newly qualified midwife in Canada, we decided the most important thing was to get our child home. In addition, the bottle feeding meant that we had a record of his minimum intake, a concern considering he weighed just over five pounds when we took him home.

DINING AT HOME (OR THERE'S NO PLACE LIKE HOME)

The day after Mothering Sunday 2006, Gabriel arrived home complete with the remaining donor human milk in a cooler box along with a prescription. For the next three months, or until Gabriel was approximately one month corrected age (or just over four months actual age), we obtained donor human milk via the bus station in Dublin to supplement Tanya's own milk, which despite expressing and feeding at the breast, never produced more than a few hundred millilitres in a day. We worked closely with the staff at the Northern Ireland milk bank whose community-based nature meant that they were able to supply us donor human milk for home consumption, a feature that hospital-based donor human milk banks are often unable to offer for legal or other reasons.

Approximately every two weeks a supply of frozen packed donor human milk would be shipped from Irvinestown in County Fermanagh to Dublin City centre via the Irish bus service, which at that time offered a courier service free of charge, reducing the costs of this invaluable medical supplement. Arriving, as we described above, in a large cooler container with ice packs around the individual bottles, the milk—once it reached our home, approximate sixteen miles to the west of Dublin—was stored in a specifically purchased small chest freezer until it was needed.

Gabriel went to Tanya's breast also on a regular basis, and she continued to express approximately eight times a day. However, she could never, despite excellent lactation support, produce a full supply of milk. Therefore, each feed was supplemented with donor human milk. Gabriel received milk from approximately thirty mothers from both sides of the border, although his main donor was a mother who had given birth around the same time, and whose infant weighed over eleven pounds. Her milk was particularly high in fat, which contributed to both her own child and Gabriel gaining weight quickly (providing reassuring evidence that milk donation is not at the expense of the health and nutrition of a donor's own child). We never knew her name as there is a general policy regarding anonymity between donors and parents of recipients. By the time Gabriel reached the date he was supposed to have been born, when he was approximately two months old, he weighed just over eight pounds, a healthy birth weight by most standards.

Gabriel continued to grow and to thrive on the limited milk Tanya was able to produce, supplemented with donor human milk. Few people, however, knew about donor human milk banks and the supplies were very limited, so we offered to use our media contacts to help in some way to obtain additional donors. Prior to her pregnancy, Tanya had been a guest on a popular Irish television program discussing women and alcohol, and she contacted them to discuss doing a program about donor human milk banking, which they thought was an astonishing and fascinating idea.

We appeared on the television program along with Gabriel (who slept peacefully through most of the discussion) and the manager of the Northern Ireland milk bank, whom we had spoken to on the telephone several times but had never met in person. She had never seen Gabriel either, and although we showed pictures from shortly after he was born, she was amazed at his current size, which at one month corrected, or four months of actual age, was over eleven pounds. The bank had another two infants in greater need of its limited supplies, so Gabriel could only receive one more shipment of donor milk. Unwittingly, therefore, Gabriel performed a very generous and sacrificial act by appearing on television: he publicized donor milk for other babies at the expense of his own supply.

ORGANIC PLEASE

The donor human milk bank did receive a number of new donors because of the media help that we provided, but supplies were still

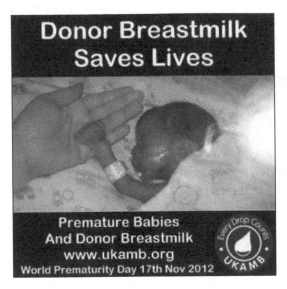

rather limited, and we had to supplement the continued meagre amounts of mother's own milk that Tanya was able to express with infant formula. In consultation with our neonatologist, we decided to use a bovine organic-based formula. Our neonatologist also suggested that we slowly introduce solids to Gabriel at this four month stage to limit the amount of formula that Gabriel would be reliant on. Gabriel continued to thrive, although his favourite food continued to be the small amounts of mother's own milk that Tanya was able to produce for him on a daily basis until he was two years old corrected (i.e., two years and two months old). We recognize that certain socio-economic advantages allow us to make choices of this kind.

At that point Tanya decided to return to research, beginning with an autoethnographic project involving narrative interviews of mothers of premature infants and their experiences with breastmilk. She also returned to doing research on donor human milk banking and to helping whenever possible to advertise milk banking, encouraging women to donate if possible. We use this picture of Gabriel holding Tanya's hand when he was just three days old to help to promote world donor milk exchange.

Tanya continues to work on issues associated with parenting and food while Gabriel grows steadily and is now physically and intellectually advanced for his years. We are reminded of how truly fortunate we are to have him in our lives. Apart from the dreams that have come true, there remain, however, the lost dreams and the occasional tears for the life that was lost in the death of our first son Liam. We both remember him and his short time with us. Our one wish is to work towards a world where infants like

Liam and Gabriel have the statistics in their favour, and that all children will have the opportunity to benefit from the health and life-giving properties of being exclusively fed human milk, at least at the beginning of their lives.

ENDNOTES

[1]Tanya has recently been awarded an EU Horizon 2020 Marie Skłodowska Curie fellowship to conduct a comparative study of donor human milk banking in the UK.

[2]On Liam's tenth birthday Conrad posted a complete story that he had previously written about our son's life and death (see https://conradbrunstrom.wordpress.com/2015/02/24/save-me-time-liams-tenth-birthday-a-complete-life/).

WORKS CITED

"Premature Birth, Aetiology, Best Practice." *British Medical Journal* (BMJ). n.d. Web. 20 August 2015.

Cassidy, Tanya M. "PumpMoms: Online Maternal Support, Social and Cultural Stigma, and Changing Technologies Associated with Breast Milk Feeding." Eds. Florence Pasche Guignard and Tanya M. Cassidy. *Mothers and Food. Negotiating Foodways from Maternal Perspectives*. Demeter Press, 2016. Print.

Cassidy, Tanya. "Ireland, Irish Women and Lactation Surrogacy: Imagining a World Where It Takes a Community to Feed a Child." Eds. Tanya M. Cassidy and Abdullahi El Tom. *Ethnographies of Breastfeeding: Cultural Contexts and Confrontations*. London: Bloomsbury Press, 2015. 45-58. Print.

Cassidy, Tanya. "'Milky Matches': Globalization, Maternal Trust, and 'Lactivist' Online Networking." *Journal of the Motherhood Initiative (JMI)* 3.2 (2012): 226-240. Print.

Cassidy, Tanya. "Mothers, Milk, and Money: Maternal Corporeal Generosity, Sociological Social Psychological Trust, and Value in Human Milk Exchange." *Journal of the Motherhood Initiative (JMI)* 3.1 (2012): 96-111. Print.

Dempsey, E. and J. Miletin. "Banked Preterm Versus Banked Term Human Milk to Promote Growth and Development in Very

Low Birth Weight Infants." *Cochrane Database of Systematic Reviews*. 6. Art. No.: CD007644.2010. Web. 20 August 2015. Moore Elizabeth R,

Anderson Gene C., Nils Bergman, and Therese Dowswell. "Early Skin-to-skin Contact for Mothers and Their Healthy Newborn Infants." *Cochrane Database Systematic Reviews* **16**.5 (2012): CD003519. Print.

Thompson Jane F., Laura J. Heal, Christine L. Roberts, and David A. Ellwood. "Women's Breastfeeding Experiences Following a Significant Primary Postpartum Haemorrhage: A Multicentre Cohort Study." *International Breastfeed Journal* 5.5. (2010):1-12 Web. 20 August 2015.

Van Esterik, Penny. "Foreword – What Flows Through Us: Re-thinking Breastfeeding as Product and Process." Eds. Tanya M. Cassidy, and Abdullahi El Tom. *Ethnographies of Breastfeeding: Cultural Contexts and Confrontations*. London: Bloomsbury Publishers, 2015. xv-xxiii. Print.

Wagner, J., C. Hanson, and A. Berry. "Donor Human Milk for Premature Infants: A Review of Current Evidence." *Infant, Child & Adolescent Nutrition* 5.2 (2013): 71-77. Print.

II.
Memories, Responsibility, and Authority

6.
Feeding Hannah

ROBIN SILBERGLEID

FEEDING MY DAUGHTER WAS THE EASIEST THING in the world. The first time I held her, just hours after they cut her from my body screaming, she latched onto my breast like a pro. No need to reposition her body or readjust her lips, she just suckled, her eyes slick as seals under her pink-and-blue-striped cap. I held her whole tiny hand wrapped around my swollen fingers and stared at her. A Kodak moment, if ever there were such a thing.

Two days later the lactation consultant came by with a young nursing student holding a clipboard trailing behind her. Like everyone else, she opened my terry-cloth robe and pressed the tops of my breasts. "You have the perfect breasts for this," she said. And she pointed out how I held Hannah, her little ear, shoulder, and buttock all in a neat row, abdomen to abdomen. Hannah's eyes fluttered and shut, so I stroked the bottoms of her long feet. She swallowed again, her small jaw working the aureole. She'd been practising for months; I'd seen her sucking her thumb on sonogram pictures and gulping the amniotic fluid she swam in. I'd practised, too, holding hard plastic dolls to my flat chest when I was seven or eight while my mother's friends nursed their babies over cookies and tea.

The consultant left Hannah and me alone in the hospital room to do what our bodies were supposed to do. On the nursery form, I recorded how many minutes Hannah drank on each side, how many diapers she soiled. I felt as if I'd just ripped open my high school grade report and found the "A" that I'd expected but couldn't be too certain about. I knew that I wouldn't be one of those women whose babies didn't know how to latch properly; one of those who didn't produce enough milk and who called the hospital crying because nobody ever said breastfeeding would be so darn hard.

From the time I saw the second blue line on the home pregnancy test, I knew it was just a matter of time before my body rejected her. The first scare came just over a week later. Fat drops of blood hit the bathroom tile like rain. I called the fertility clinic and they brought me in for an early sonogram, just as they'd done months before when I was pregnant and woke to red. But there it was glowing on the monitor: a balloon no bigger than a child's fingernail, a gestational sac.

For now that was enough.

At seventeen weeks, I was convinced I was leaking amniotic fluid and ended up in the labour and delivery ward. I wasn't, at least according to the doctor who saw me that worry-filled night. Within a week, the leaking had stopped and I found out the child swimming around in my uterus was a girl.

At thirty-one weeks, I started having regular contractions, ironically enough during the tour of the hospital that concluded our childbirth class. The obstetrician sent me home to rest and told me to come back in when I had more than six contractions in an hour. I spent the next seven weeks counting.

If I wasn't counting contractions, I was counting kicks. If I played Sheryl Crow in the car, the baby would wiggle, but my doctor couldn't get her to move for anything during our routine non-stress tests. She sent me across the street to the labour and delivery ward for monitoring. I spent one more weekend pregnant, couch bound, and counting.

After Cytotec, Pitocin, and an amniotomy, they cut Hannah screaming from my body. I spent most of the twenty-one hours of labour doing what I swore that I wouldn't do: watching the steady rate of her heart and the peaks and valleys of my contractions on the monitor. By the time they let me nurse Hannah in the recovery room, I was truly amazed that she was mine to keep, that we'd made it through thirty-eight weeks more or less intact.

Those first days home were delicious—my own mother in the kitchen cooking roast beef and mashed potatoes while I sat on the couch and nursed. Every afternoon she came home with grocery bags full of frozen fruit and soy milk for smoothies, whole chickens and leafy greens. Friends brought us French onion soup and *arroz con pollo*. I ate. And my daughter drank. Slow, deep sips of milk from my breasts.

At her two-week check-up, she had gained back her birth weight and more. The paediatrician smiled, touched Hannah's chin, and said: "Your mommy makes some really good milk." I took her home, pleased. Every two hours I opened my blouse and let her drink. And every two hours, she pooped. Her stool was so loose it pooled in the diaper and leaked onto the changing table or floor. Soiled sleepers and onesies soaked in cold water in the bathroom sink. The paediatrician reassured me that Hannah was thriving. But if I was worried, she said, I could stop eating all dairy products and beef.

I did. Nothing changed.

I accepted the mustard-coloured stains on her clothing as a normal part of mothering, just as I accepted the hours of walking a colicky baby, Hannah strapped to my chest in a carrier, her small feet kicking the top of my thighs. And I assumed—I had to assume—that one day I'd look in Hannah's diaper and see what all the books said I was supposed to see. In the meantime, I mothered her. I held her, nursed her, rocked her, and changed her.

Then I found blood in her diaper.

Hannah was almost four months. Those colicky weeks—the days she cried what seemed to be literally nonstop—seemed to be behind us. Her reflux was more or less under control on Zantac. She seemed to be settling into a nap schedule. As long as she ate every two to three hours, I could take her anywhere. I timed trips to the city so that she napped in the car both ways. I spent my first Mother's Day changing Hannah's diapers and my clothes. Once again, a few flecks of blood changed my life.

Since her diapers tested positive for occult blood, she was given a prescription for the reflux drug Prevacid. I didn't quite understand how controlling Hannah's reflux would stop intestinal bleeding, but I took the doctor's word for it and dutifully force-fed her an ounce of thick, pink liquid every day. Small white granules floated in the medicine like stars. They clogged the nipples of her bottles;

I sucked them up with a dropper and placed them on Hannah's tongue. She still vomited, now an obscene orangey-pink colour. And still she bled.

A parent of the Internet age, I perused websites and abstracts on medical research databases. I read that the most common reason for rectal bleeding in infants is allergy, and since I had already cut the top allergen (cow's milk) from my diet, I proceeded down the list. Many children allergic to dairy are also allergic to soy. Eggs, nuts, and wheat also cause problems for many infants. I was convinced that she was allergic to strawberries, citrus fruits, tomatoes, and corn. For weeks, I ate from a list of the most hypoallergenic foods. I called lactation consultants and researched paediatric gastroenterologists in our area. A woman I know said something similar had happened to her son and he spent six weeks in the hospital. They never figured out what was wrong, but today he's a healthy three-year-old who still nurses at bedtime. I wondered if it wasn't an allergy at all. I wondered if it was Crohn's disease or colitis. I checked Hannah compulsively for dehydration, feeling the top of her pulsing skull. But except for the leaky, blood-streaked diapers, she appeared to be thriving, more than doubling her birth weight at four months.

I read in an essay on haemorrhagic colitis in breastfed infants that "evolution after maternal diet is, as usual, simple," which I took to mean she would outgrow her problems once we weaned and she began to eat solid food. Those words tore at me as my milk ravaged Hannah's digestive system. Still, I kept nursing her. Everything told me "breast was best," even advertisements for baby formula, parenting guides, and paediatricians. I was her mother. What else could I do?

I wasn't one of those women who wanted to breastfeed her child through preschool or beyond. I always assumed that I'd easily breastfeed, and I always assumed that once her first birthday arrived I would gracefully, gratefully, wean. I wasn't one of those women who thought nursing was particularly sensual. At times, I resented the tugging on my nipples. At times, I resented my body being so intimately responsible for hers. But most of the time I nursed her in the same way I approached the rest of motherhood: she was my daughter and I couldn't separate her needs from my own. All I knew was in the mere four months since the doctor violently severed our bodies on the operating table, the prospect of not breastfeeding her filled me with a sadness that I couldn't articulate.

In late June, when Hannah was nearly five months, we drove the familiar highway to yet another doctor at yet another Dallas hospital. She slept the entire way, while I wondered if the gastroenterologist would take one look at her and tell me she needed to be on hypoallergenic formula. My hands left sweaty prints on the steering wheel. In the waiting room, a mother of triplet boys was talking about going through multiple surgeries. Two of the boys played with multicoloured toys strung on the handles of their carriers. The other one, pale with dark, unwashed hair, crawled on the floor over to us. The air around him reeked of something that I couldn't name. Hannah fussed in her stroller, and I glanced at the clock. When I sat her on my lap, she turned her head, toward my breasts heavy with longing. The triplets and their mother followed a nurse to an examination room, and I sniffed the top of Hannah's head. She smelled like me. Finally, her nurse, a scruffy, pony-tailed man, called us back for her appointment.

I was so sure the doctor would recommend formula feeding that what he did say caught me completely off guard: nine times out of ten, the diagnosis for a child with Hannah's condition is food allergy. From there he proceeded to tell me that if I wanted to continue nursing my daughter, I should eat nothing but fresh fruit, vegetables, and meats. No processed foods, no restaurant foods, no meals that I didn't prepare. Allergens hid everywhere. Even a fruit salad at a friend's potluck could be inadvertently splashed with ranch dressing from someone's salad. Even my prenatal vitamins could be contaminated. I never got a chance to ask if it was possible something else was wrong. The doctor assured me that if I did what he said Hannah would be symptom-free within a month.

When we were alone in the examining room, I gave her my left breast. I wondered if the fish I'd eaten the week before was cooked in butter. I wondered how many allergens she swallowed each feeding. I broke the suction of Hannah's lips with my finger and put her clothes back on. At the checkout counter, the receptionist gave me a copy of the doctor's scrawled instructions—Diet: Breast-feeding. Medicine: Zantac. Follow-up: Two months.

On the way home, we stopped at Whole Foods. With a receiving blanket over my shoulder and Hannah's hand on the bare skin under my t-shirt, I ate a meagre salad and nursed her in the café. We both ate greedily. Then she slept in her carrier while I filled the cart with organic poultry and lamb, Granny Smith apples and sweet potatoes, pound after pound of rice, one of the only grains that I could eat. I remembered the doctor's words as the grains poured into plastic sacks: "No label. It's just rice." I turned recipes over in my mind. Tonight, chicken with roasted vegetables. Tomorrow, lamb chops and steamed carrots. And in a month, Hannah would be well.

Buying organic produce at Whole Foods was the first step in what I'd fondly come to think of as my sweet potato fantasy. In those long months when I wondered if I'd ever have a healthy child, I would see the owner of a local cafe feeding her toddler sweet potatoes—not from a glass Gerber jar or even from Tupperware containers like everyone that I knew. No, this woman scooped tiny spoonfuls straight from the skin into her daughter's mouth. And when she was through, she carried the sleepy child over her shoulder and placed her in a playpen in the back corner. The scene encapsulated all my fondest images of motherhood. I wanted to feed Hannah sweet potatoes. I wanted to take her to farmers' markets and let her pick the reddest, ripest tomatoes for our salads. I wanted to teach her how to make latkes for the holidays. I wanted lazy weekend mornings with French toast and real maple syrup. But I wondered if I'd ever share a meal with my daughter.

I'd be lying if I said that I did exactly what the doctor had ordered. I did eat packaged food. But I figured a PhD in literature should enable me to determine that "rye, water, salt," or "potatoes, sunflower oil, salt" didn't have any of what I affectionately referred to as "the big eight allergens." It seemed to work. Three separate diapers checked negative for occult blood. Even though her stool was still too runny, there was little reason to believe she wasn't going to be fine.

For the first time in months, I accepted an invitation for dinner. Chicken and rice for me, spicy beef tacos for the hosts. When my friend assured me the taco consisted of only beef, pepper, onion, and garlic—all things I'd eaten before—I had a second helping of meat and rice. Within an hour I had a headache, a clear sign that the food was laced with preservatives. The next day, Hannah had the worst diarrhoea of her life, and she never got back to anything resembling better.

In September, I took Hannah for allergy testing. If only I knew what foods bothered her, I could cut them easily from my diet. She had bad days and worse days, and I was sure she had an allergy to something that I ate on a regular basis such as rice or potatoes. The allergist's office was just down the hall from the gastroen-terologist's, in the children's wing of a major medical center. We sat with one girl hooked up to an IV and a little boy waiting for respiratory therapy. Hannah crawled on the carpeted floor and flirted with the nurses.

I dutifully checked boxes on the twelve-page form: runny nose, watery eyes, vomiting, diarrhoea. We didn't have roaches, but we did live near a wooded area. Allergen covers on my mattress, but not hers. No definite food allergies but many suspected. Reacted badly to rice cereal. Currently, exclusively breastfed.

"What a pretty dress, Hannah," the allergist cooed before asking me to elaborate on Hannah's medical history.

The doctor listened and typed my answers into the computer. "Honestly," she said, "this doesn't sound like an allergy to me. Or, frankly, any type of food hypersensitivity. You've been avoiding all major allergens for two months. And it hasn't made any difference."

"But..." I hesitated. "Dr. Chang said he was sure that it is an allergy. Isn't it worth testing her?"

"I'm definitely not going to put her through a skin test. When do you see Dr. Chang again?"

"Next week."

"Why don't you try cutting rice? Can you do that?" She paused. "Just for a week?"

From research I had done on breastfeeding allergic kids, I knew that one week wasn't long enough to observe any change. It would take at least two weeks, possibly even a month, for all the rice to pass through my milk and out of Hannah, if indeed rice was the culprit. "Yes," I said. "I can do that."

But I was hungry all the time. I weighed less than I did when I got pregnant, less than I did when I was studying for my PhD qualifying exams, less than I did when I started high school and my mother worried about anorexia. There was no question that breastfeeding was taking its toll on me, too.

"You really don't think it's worth testing her?" I said to the allergist. I know that I sounded desperate.

"Okay, let's do this. I'll write up a requisition to have her blood tested for common allergens and rice. You can have it done next week. I'm sure Dr. Chang will want to do some tests on her and it doesn't make sense to stick her twice. Does that sound reasonable?"

"Yes." I could wait a week. But I asked her to add potatoes, oats, and rye to the list.

"I really don't expect any positive results. What I can tell you is in all the cases of chronic diarrhoea and blood in the stool that I've seen—even when we never figure out what causes it—it always goes away."

It was me, not Hannah, who cried the whole way home.

Eight days later, Hannah had her first bottle of hypoallergenic formula. Fourteen days later, the nurse called to say that all her allergy tests came back negative.

I wasn't ready to wean Hannah, still months shy of her first birthday. But she was ready to eat something other than my milk. The child who'd always refused to take a bottle from me drank twelve ounces of formula the first day that I offered it to her. It smelled awful. It tasted worse. It left a grainy film on her bottles. The stench of her diapers made me gag, and I remembered the little boy crawling around at Dr. Chang's office. Even the website for Hannah's formula—Neocate, available prescription only—said that parents might notice a change in their child's "wind." But she drank. In two days she had the first normal stool of her life. She was seven months old.

At daycare, she downed bottles of formula, twenty-four ounces during the day, and nursed peacefully at night. I spent over an hour a day attached to the breast pump. The milk let down every two hours, and my breasts throbbed from plugged ducts. Still, I wasn't taking chances. I'd heard in an Internet support group for parents of kids with food allergies that sometimes even these amino-acid-based formulas don't work, and babies need to go back to breast milk while their mothers' diets whittle down to two or three foods or even elemental formula. I wanted to be sure the formula worked; I wasn't ready to wean. At night, I tucked cloth diapers in my shirts to soak up the milk that Hannah didn't drink. Her paediatrician told me not to worry; I could go on breastfeeding as long as I wanted. "Just look at her," she said at Hannah's six month appointment. "She's healthy. She's developing right on schedule." Lactation consultants told me the same thing: "As long as she's gaining weight, you should be able to continue nursing." But the first words out of her gastroenterologist's mouth at her checkup chided me: "I hope you're not still breastfeeding her."

Clearly, he said, I hadn't followed his diet. There was no other explanation for why Hannah still had diarrhoea, why she'd recently had another incidence of rectal bleeding. I gratefully accepted the free cans of formula and didn't bother scheduling another appointment.

For several agonizing weeks, I debated the pros and cons of breastfeeding part time and pumping milk to save for later use. There was no denying Hannah was getting better on the formula. But was she 100 percent better? My diet was the same as it had been, which meant I was still eating something that had ravaged her digestive system. Yet, as her paediatrician and everyone else insisted, from the perspective of immunity and development, "breast is best." I couldn't imagine lying next to my child at night and not nursing her when she cried. And I wanted to eat.

I craved chocolate cake. I remembered when I was pregnant with Hannah that I had seen a commercial on TV and decided I needed to have chocolate cake. Immediately. I wanted the cake so badly that I pulled a coat on over my pajamas and drove ten minutes to the grocery store; at home, I ate until I fell into soothing chocolate dreams. Now, I stared at chocolate cream pies at our local gourmet shop. I told Hannah that I wanted a tuna melt and chicken lo mein. I wanted pad thai and pepperoni pizza. I wanted to eat without thinking about ingredients.

But I wanted to nurse my daughter.

In the end, my decision came down to simple math. The risks no longer outweighed the benefits for either one of us. Neocate was helping her while my "elimination diet" was starving me. We were down to two feedings a night. I stopped dragging the breast pump to work. But as long as I nursed her, my body would keep producing milk; we could go on like that for years. In the end, it was Hannah who convinced me: I found another runny stool in her diaper. I didn't want to wonder anymore if it was my fault. The doctor's words gnawed my stomach like an ulcer.

The last time I nursed my daughter she was a week shy of nine months. I held her in the rocking chair while she suckled, her two new teeth scraping the underside of my nipple. Her fat hand pulsed against my chest. If I'd known that it would definitely be the last time, perhaps I would have paid more attention. Perhaps I would have nursed her longer until both breasts drained and she fell into satiated sleep. As it happened, it was uneventful. When she stopped swallowing, I replaced my nipple with her pacifier and laid her in the crib. Maybe I went into the kitchen to wash dishes. Maybe I sat down in front of the television to catch the news. I really don't remember. Later, when she woke for food, I gave her a bottle.

In the morning, Hannah was weaned. I dropped her off at daycare and went to Starbucks where I sipped coffee (caffeine, milk, sugar) and savoured lemon pound cake (milk, wheat, egg). At lunch, I ate a turkey sandwich and consumed enough allergens that I knew I wouldn't consider nursing Hannah for another two weeks. Maybe, I told myself. Maybe we'd eat sweet potatoes together at Thanksgiving.

7.
Farm Culture, the Politics of Food, and Maternal Guilt

B. LEE MURRAY

I'M SURE THAT EVERYONE SAW ME RUNNING around like a crazy and possessed woman. Some people said that I worked too hard, but I was never sure what I should take from that comment. My mom tried to help out, but we never discussed my frenzied existence. It seemed to be the accepted way things were on a farm. All the work and all the money were about the farm. I grew up on a farm knowing and thinking that the farm was the priority and any work off the farm was to subsidize the farm. Our farm included cereal crops, a market garden, a greenhouse, a grain cleaning plant, a large farmyard to maintain, poultry, canning, cleaning, and children. I also worked off the farm in the field of nursing.

Mothering was in the spaces, in the margins, and sometimes simultaneous with the work. I think my children worked too hard, too. This again was part of living on a farm, or so I thought and so I was led to believe. I grew up with the work ethic of the importance of the farm and the ultimate goal of getting the crop off. I carried on with that philosophy in my married life. That philosophy was occasionally challenged by people whom I thought just didn't understand.

I wanted to feed my children wholesome and organic food, which included breastfeeding them until at least a year old and giving them homegrown food following. All the vegetables, meat and bread they ate were produced on the farm and many of the fruits as well. This continued throughout their childhood and my daughter, now an adult, recalls longing for a white bread sandwich and a Fruit Roll-Up in her lunch instead of a whole wheat ground homemade

83

bread sandwich and fresh or canned fruit and vegetables grown and prepared on the farm. And trust me, sometimes I would have loved to toss in some prepared food and treats and spend my time doing other things. But I would have felt too guilty; besides I wanted the best for my children. The farm culture and the media told me exactly what was expected of me when providing optimum nutrition to my children and how to be a "good mom" in that department.

No one told me how difficult it was to provide homegrown nutritious wholesome food to my children 24/7. The first three years trying to sow, tend, reap, and can the produce from a large garden were a disaster as I tried to cope with drought, hail, nasty insects, and weeds. I felt guilty for wanting to quit, and I didn't want to tell anyone how badly I wanted to stop trying to feed my children only the very best of food. It was so time consuming and frustrating at times, and I felt as if I was neglecting my children in other ways, but I carried on and tried to do it all. I kept my feelings a secret, and the seeds of resentment were planted.

GUILT, SECRETS AND DECEPTION

I brought three children into the frenzied existence of farm life. I grew up seeing my mom do it, so I knew what to do. I also had my mom nearby to coach me, support me, and assist me. I never talked to her or to anyone else about the difficulty of trying to do it all. I worked very hard at keeping that secret mostly because of guilt but also because I thought I must have some type of flaw. I thought there was something wrong with me and that I needed to try harder, be more organized, and appreciate our healthy lifestyle. But how healthy was it if all my time was spent working and not playing with or enjoying my children?

I lost myself somewhere along the way and only found myself when I was mothering. I never could find, however, the time to mother the way I needed to stay whole. And, most of all, I didn't know that I could quit or at least use some processed foods and the world would not collapse. The weeds might have grown, the fruit may have rotted or dried up, and I may have disappointed my husband and my family, but regret would not have been such a big part of my memory of mothering during that time and place.

I felt unhappy and discontent but mostly shameful for feeling the way I did.

I kept that secret for a long time. I told no one. But did I intentionally conceal the fact that I was unhappy, or was I also deceiving myself? On one hand, I inherently knew that I was unhappy, but I did not trust my own thoughts or feelings. Petrarch stated that self-deception may be "the most deadly thing in life" and continued:

> O race of mortal men, this it is that above all makes me astonished and fearful for you, when I behold you, of your own free will, clinging to your miseries; pretending that you do not know the peril hanging over your heads, and if one brings it under your very eyes, you try to thrust it from your sight and put it far off. (Petrarch qtd. in Bok 59)

And so I clung to my miseries. I tried to ignore the unsettledness, the wariness, the shame, and most of all the discontent. I told myself that I was just ungrateful; I should be happy; I could be happy if only I tried harder. I tried to wear the happy mask, but I was only deceiving myself. I tried to push unhappiness out of my sight.

I don't think my intention was to deceive anyone else. To intentionally deceive would require awareness, and I had not recognized this discontent as real or acceptable. Freud speaks of "false consciousness"—a lack of awareness of our hidden or unconscious feelings and thoughts— and "defense mechanisms"—an unconscious denial of reality to avoid anxiety and he maintained that our self-illusions stand in the way of becoming free: "Only through unmasking, demystification, above all interpretation, can we break through the web of illusion and become aware of our role in perpetuating it" (Bok 60). I was not aware of this unconscious denial of my reality. I maintained an illusion of contentment and happiness and was unable to name the emptiness I felt. My deception, although unconscious to some degree, was getting in the way of me processing and making sense of my reality, my situation, and my circumstances. I always felt torn between time with my children and time tending the garden.

However, Freud also discussed defense mechanisms as a means of survival or protecting ourselves from a truth we cannot accept or cannot face. And so we keep that truth a secret mostly from ourselves in the form of repressed knowledge. We are both inside and outside this experience. We hide something that we are not sure exists or perhaps we do not recognize as existing. Self-deception related to secrecy is confusing to our conscious and unconscious mind. How can we hide something that we are literally in the dark about?

Was I being deceiving or being deceived? Was my mask held in place by self-deception or fear? Which one kept the mask on most? Which one was responsible for my behaviour? Which one kept me stuck? I had a deep sense of being a "bad" mother regardless of what I did. I struggled constantly to try to do it all, and yet it seemed that I was failing on all counts.

I had a strong sense of my unhappiness, but I also blamed myself for that unhappiness. I felt unappreciative of my three wonderful children, my health, my family, my job, and my friends. I repeatedly told myself I should be happy. There were many people less fortunate than me. It was shameful to be so self-centered and unappreciative. I should have been able to think about all those good things and make myself happy and content. But how could I have been happy all the time? Everyone has her "down days," and since there were good times, I could always rationalize that I could or should be happier. I convinced myself it was a matter of willpower and attitude.

The words unhappy, sad, and bored were not part of our vocabulary as a family when I was growing up. I always felt guilty as a child and adolescent if I voiced those negative emotions. I never learned how to express those emotions, but I learned how to pretend they didn't exist. There was never a conversation about feeling bad or sad, but there were conversations about why I should be happy. I learned how to deny those negative feelings and put on a happy face. I wore a mask, but I don't remember putting it on. I didn't think there was anyone to tell about how I felt without feeling some degree of shame or failure.

FARM CULTURE AND THE POLITICS OF FOOD

The local farm culture of the Canadian prairies dictated the expectations of farm women, their role on the farm, and their role as a mother. There was also an expectation that children should work on the farm and work should come before play. These expectations influenced my values and beliefs about what was most important for my children, and the local farm politics related to food production promoted what was considered healthy food and what was not. The land, resources, and equipment were available to have homegrown organic food, so any other options were not acceptable. We were not financially stable and I believed at that time that I was providing wholesome food at the best price possible.

The farm work ethic I grew up with was getting in my way now. I truly believed that I needed to have the garden weeded, to have three home-cooked meals a day prepared with fresh produce, to have the other farm work done, and to have integrated mothering with the farm work. There was no time for play for anyone, and yet the expectation was that I should enjoy it and embrace it. People would say, "How do you do it all?" I thought that they were giving me a compliment. I took some pride in "doing it all" and the busyness kept me from consciously thinking about the discontent.

I didn't realize until much later that the busyness served a purpose. It became part of the denial. If I could stay busy, I didn't have time to think. I could go from one task to the next without stopping to recognize how I was feeling—without recognizing what was going on around me. I was always completing one job so that I could move onto the next. By being busy enough, always planning for the next step, I didn't let my mind wander; I neither had the time nor the energy to reflect on where I was in life and where I wanted to be.

I could put things in their separate little boxes and keep parts of my life separate from the rest. My outside life was very organized—minute by minute, hour by hour— and planned to accomplish the many tasks just in the allotted time. When the unforeseen happened, it meant frantic reorganization to establish equilibrium once again. If I could keep my outside life organized, I didn't have to look at the messiness on the inside and the looming discontent.

Everyone around me looked happier than me, yet no one knew I was unhappy, and I sure wasn't going to tell.

Instinctively I knew I was unsettled. My intuition told me that something was not right. If I stopped long enough, I would get a glimpse of how I wished things could be. If I stopped long enough, I would try to satisfy my instincts and intuition and that scared me even more. What would happen if I did things differently? What would happen if I stopped sowing, growing, tending, and preserving this wonderful and valuable food? What would the dangers and consequences be of following my intuition? I guess I needed to do something, but I didn't know what it was I needed to do. I also did not trust my intuition, and I was still convinced that I was being ungrateful—that wanting more or something different was betraying someone or something. But I still felt that I needed to be doing something different; I needed to spend more time with my children in a more relaxed and playful way.

I remember this time as fragments of memory, scattered and frenzied, always organizing time to make room to work: room to work in the yard, the garden, the house, the barn ... never organizing time to spend with my children away from the yard, the garden, the house, the barn. The same fragments of memory keep flashing back.

I wind up the swing chair one more time and rush outside to do more hoeing and weeding. His head looks crinkled, and I wonder if babies get stiff necks if they sleep with their head flopped to the side, but if I move his head he may wake up and I will not get the gardening done. He is only six months old.

She is so excited that we are going to the lake today. She knows we need to get the hoeing and weeding done first, and she is more than happy to help. First, it is the garden and then the trees and soon the day is fading away, and we never get to the lake. She is only nine years old.

I see him through the greenhouse window reflected in the morning sun. He is playing in the sandbox with his toys and looks so sweet and innocent. I want to rush out to hug him and play with him.

I just need to finish the transplanting, but then it is bedtime. His little brother will be born soon. He is only five years old.

I leave him at nursery school, and he is crying as usual. The "experts" have told me that it is good for children with special needs to go to school early and learn from their peers. I rush back to the farm to get my gardening and chores done. He is only four years old.

She is upset and bewildered when her mom is so distraught. She tries to comfort me to make me happy. Nothing seems to work. She is only twelve years old.

He has been practising all day. I see only glimpses of him as he goes by the greenhouse on his little motorbike. He comes into the greenhouse and asks me to come out and watch him do a jump. He revs his motor and approaches his homemade ramp. I hold my breath, and at the last moment he lets off the throttle and plunges head first into the dirt. He cries and I console him. How do I tell him that life is about knowing when to let off the throttle and when to take a risk? I wish I could tell him the difference. He is only ten years old.

It was a double-edged sword. If I continued to provide this whole-some, homegrown food to my children I would not have time to spend with them in other ways and they would continue to work alongside me rather than playing as children are supposed to play. And if I quit or cut back on the gardening, preserving, cooking, baking and tending to the animals, my children would be deprived of the healthy lifestyle they deserved. Or so I believed. I felt a lot of guilt and resentment and I repressed any anger I may have felt as a result of my frustration. Lerner makes a fitting analogy about mothering and gardening:

> One of the things you will learn on the job (of mothering) is guilt. You may feel guilty about leaving your children for your work and guilty about leaving your work for your children. You will no doubt also feel guilty about feeling

> guilty. But try to remember that our society encourages mothers to cultivate guilt like a little flower garden, because nothing blocks the awareness and expression of legitimate anger as effectively as this all-consuming emotion. (75)

And I did feel guilty on both counts, so I tried to do both and the busyness continued.

I feel as if I have always been too busy with other things to be able to mother the way that I want to and the way I think I should. I have been like many other mothers who fool themselves by getting caught in the *after* myth: "*After* I get the dishes done, *after* I get the laundry done, *after* I get the yard and garden tended to, *after* I get the mortgage paid off, *after* I finish my education THEN I will mother the way I want to and feel I should. *After,* I will spend time with my children; I will be there when they need me; I will enjoy them and have fun with them." It is a myth because *after* never seems to come.

When I was so busy when my children were very young, I did believe that it might end someday. I believed that someday I would have time. I look back now on that time in my life and realize just how fast the treadmill was going, and I am surprised I did not slip off the back and crash. But I didn't and I am here to tell my story so that other mothers may learn a sense of balance among work, play, and mothering. We can do it all but just in smaller doses, and we do not need to do it all ourselves. When it comes to proper nutrition for our children we are caught in the spider's web of wanting and needing to provide our children with a healthy lifestyle including the very best nutrition we can, but also wanting and needing to spend time with our children in a carefree environment, which they so richly deserve. I realize now that nothing would have happened to my children if I had "cheated" and given them less nutritious food on occasion, but I was influenced by the farm culture of the time and by the politics of food production, consumption, and opportunity. It was not something to walk away from easily or without guilt.

This chapter was adapted from my PhD dissertation. Please see:

Murray, B. Lee, Secrets of Mothering, *Diss. University of Saskatchewan, 2010. Print.*

WORKS CITED

Bok, Sisella. *Secrets: On the Ethics of Concealment and Revelation.* New York: Vintage, 1989. Print.

Freud, Sigmund. *A General Introduction to Psychoanalysis.* 1935. New York: Washington Square Press, 1960. Print.

Freud, Sigmund. *The Standard Edition of the Complete Psychological Works of Sigmund Freud.* 1939. London: Hogarth Press, 1963. Print.

Lerner, Harriet. *The Mother Dance: How Children Change Your Life.* New York: HarperCollins, 1998. Print.

8.
When Feeding Your Family
Is a Full-time Job

KARI O'DRISCOLL

I GREW UP FIRMLY IN THE MIDDLE of the Pop-Tart generation. I was eight years old in 1979 when my parents divorced and my mom suddenly found herself supporting three kids after having been a full-time stay-at-home mom for more than a decade. She promptly went out and got herself a bank teller job and tried to figure out how to make ends meet. Fortunately, the supermarket was stocked with cheap convenience foods specifically marketed to working mothers. These miracles of chemistry promised to provide nutrition on a budget and soon our pantry was full of "enriched" white bread, sickeningly sweet breakfast cereals that promised to deliver all the nutrients that we needed for a great start to the day (so long as we added milk), value-packs of Frito Lay chips for school lunches, and giant jars of chunky peanut butter. The microwave quickly became the most used tool in our kitchen, accomplishing everything from "nuking" frozen waffles to heating up jet-puffed marshmallows to stuff in our after school s'mores, to cooking entire dinners. To be fair, my mom used her Crock-Pot a great deal to make chilli and spaghetti sauce, and she always made a salad with dinner, but as groceries got more expensive and my siblings and I continued to grow, the cheap, prepared stuff got easier to buy. It saved time and money, and we had no idea it was full of pesticides and fertilizers that might eventually take a toll on our developing bodies. We believed that anything on the supermarket shelves was safe, from the BPA-lined (Bisphenol A) cans of peas to the Wonder Bread that contained fifteen different ingredients that we couldn't pronounce. It had to be safe, right?

This was America. We had yet to learn about deceptive marketing terms like "natural" or "enriched" or "essential amino acids." We hadn't entertained the notion that large corporations were writing their own rules and playing around with ingredients that had no business being in food. We had no idea that we were pumping ourselves full of salt, sugar, fat, and preservatives. We didn't ask questions. We didn't know that we should have.

I did change my eating habits somewhat in college, mostly in order to avoid gaining the dreaded "Freshman 15," but I also suffered from the twenty-something invincibility syndrome that said I had plenty of time to change my habits to prevent cancer or diabetes or obesity. In my late twenties, I got pregnant and my relationship with food morphed into something else altogether. The responsibility that came along with feeding a developing child weighed heavily on my food choices. In addition to giving up alcohol upon first seeing that pink plus sign on the pregnancy test, I changed my Starbucks order to a *decaf* double tall latte and gazed longingly at the wedge of brie on my husband's plate.

I was totally committed to ensuring that I did what was best for our child and obsessively sought out parenting books and blogs. Before our baby even started kicking around in my belly, my husband Sean and I debated the merits and drawbacks of co-sleeping, pacifiers, and cloth diapers. I was firm in my decision to breastfeed, and I was lucky to be pregnant at a time when breastfeeding was the most acceptable form of nutrition for a newborn, according to the vast majority of my family and friends and medical professionals, not to mention random strangers and mommy bloggers.

It turned out that the decision to breastfeed was the last simple choice that I made regarding feeding my child. As my pregnancy progressed, I discovered intense debates regarding when exactly it is best to begin feeding your infant solid foods, which foods are the best to feed them—homemade? organic? fruit or vegetables first?—and how solid food may or may not fit in with a weaning schedule. My paediatrician had one set of guidelines based on his vast years of experience; friends who were new mothers said something slightly different; and the woman who ran the classes at the hospital had yet another perspective. It was nearly impossible to find two sources who agreed. I worried that I was in over my head. How would I ever decide what to feed my baby and when? The rising incidence of reports on toxic materials in our food supply and containers (such as BPA in plastics) raised red flags about every aspect of food from growing practices to packaging to whether or not I should feed my baby or let her feed herself. How was I to sort out all of this information?

When I was in high school, Home Economics was a popular class and a few nuggets of wisdom stuck with me over the years. In my college studies of biology and chemistry, my understanding of carbohydrates and proteins and the amino acids necessary for human life expanded. In my twenties, I dabbled in vegetarianism, which spurred me to dig deeper into just how much protein a person needed and which plants were the best sources of protein. I took solace in the notion that at least I had a rudimentary knowledge of what foods were beneficial and which ones had absolutely no redeeming value whatsoever beyond the fact that they tasted really damn good (french fries from Wendy's dipped in a frosty, anyone?).

My first daughter, Erin, was born and I muddled through, feeling confused and anxious much of the time. I had another little girl two years later and learned, among other things, how expensive organic baby food could be and exactly how long it took to find, cook, purée, and feed homemade baby food to a hungry kid. I experimented a lot, wasted a great deal of food, and finally settled into what I hoped was a pretty good compromise of avoiding the most dangerous "conventionally grown" foods and balancing the warring factions of healthy eating with time management.

Despite all of my efforts to wade through the glut of information and advice, something was off. Both my girls had been healthy, robust, average-sized newborns. I breastfed them both exclusively before beginning solid food, but between their first and second birthdays, they both slid from the fiftieth percentile of the growth chart to the fifth and stayed there. Their paediatrician was curious, but not alarmed, and I was told to pay even more attention to what I fed them and to stay away from dairy products with added growth hormones and to try to always buy organic produce. I was vigilant about feeding them enough protein, and I made sure their meals contained a balance of carbohydrates, protein, fibre, and fresh vegetables.

This was the early 2000s, and I was just beginning to tune in to conversations about locavores and sustainability and genetically modified organisms. After several years of struggling with my own odd, unexplained gastrointestinal issues, I sought out the help of a naturopath who diagnosed me with a severe gluten allergy. Shortly thereafter, my youngest daughter, Lauren, was given the same diagnosis and within weeks, her sister Erin was too.

Within three months of eliminating gluten from their diet, both of my girls grew two inches and gained enough weight to make the leap back into the fiftieth percentile on the growth chart. Erin's nervous habit of picking the skin off of her lips disappeared, and Lauren stopped grinding her teeth and complaining of near-constant headaches and stomach aches. The changes in my health were even more significant. I was sold. Gluten was the enemy. Gone were the girls' favourite Costco treats—chicken nuggets and organic macaroni and cheese. The pantry was cleared out of goldfish crackers and pretzels and stocked with nuts and dried fruit.

But it wasn't that simple. How do you know if there is gluten in something? I found myself hip-deep in a morass of information. It took me months to figure out the myriad alternate names for gluten—"glutamate," "maltodextrin," "natural flavours"—and hours and hours of reading labels in the supermarket and looking up things online. Spending a day or two in agony once or twice a month learning about cross-contamination and other gluten-containing foods, such as malt and barley, we all suffered setbacks despite my vigilance. In the end, I decided it was much safer if I made the vast majority of our food at home, but with two growing children, that was a tall order. It took me three years to come up with a healthy flour blend that didn't taste like sawdust. I was prompted to do so even with new gluten-free flour blends and products entering the market almost weekly because a little investigation revealed that the vast majority of these mixes and products had very little nutritional value. They were packed with simple starches, and I was trying to make sure my kids ate whole grain foods with fibre. Six years later, I have a system that works for us most of the time, but it is nearly a full-time job to craft healthy, tasty meals for a family of four that don't include allergens or pesticides or potentially harmful genetically modified organisms (GMOs).

Every Saturday evening, I go over the calendar for the coming week, noting school days and extra activities, such as gymnastics or basketball. I scour cookbooks and family recipes for dinner ideas and put together a grocery list. Sundays generally find me at two or three different grocery stores and a farmer's market getting everything on my list. Although we are lucky enough to live in a big city, not all of the stores carry the products that I am looking for—almond flour or grass-fed beef or the gluten-free crackers that the girls like. Sunday afternoons are generally spent making staples that we need for the coming week such as gluten-free baguettes or muffins for weekday breakfasts and devilled eggs for snacks. Daily, I spend a minimum of two hours preparing meals, including school lunches and dinner. If one of my children is invited to a schoolmate's party, I try to whip up a batch of gluten-free cupcakes or cookies to send with her so that she won't be left out of the celebration.

I read food blogs a few times a week to find new recipes and to keep up on the latest research. It is both fun and exhausting. I was sad to learn that most of the corn sold in the United States is genetically modified not only because I am not convinced that GMOs are safe but also because it means I have to work harder to find only organic, non-GMO corn for my family and avoid products that use GMO corn or cornstarch. When information about high arsenic levels in rice appeared in several news outlets, I was shaken. As a gluten-free household, we rely a lot on rice and rice flours, and the solution isn't as simple as finding organic rice because even organic rice has arsenic in it. It was back to the drawing board to convince my family to try quinoa or buckwheat or other grains that are (so far as I know) safer. I felt safe with organic produce until I read that even organic apples and pears have been treated with antibiotics to curb the devastation of blight.

I swapped all of our plastic food containers for glass ones a few years ago after reading about the increased evidence that BPA was harmful. I still avoid plastics because I figure if it was easy for the plastic manufacturers to use BPA, whether they knew it could cause problems or not, who is to say that whatever they replaced it with wouldn't be just as bad. I can only hope that they don't discover something horrifyingly toxic in glass one day.

The research and constant barrage of information is often overwhelming—food as medicine, Michael Pollan and the slow-food movement, entire channels on cable TV devoted to cooking and food. It is terrifically difficult and time consuming to sort out science from fad and, all the while, my children are growing and developing and wondering why I won't buy Nacho Cheese Doritos and stock the pantry with cookies as a lot of their friends' parents do.

My Facebook and Twitter feeds are crowded with testimonials about sugar fasts and the Paleo diet, the newest research on heavy metals in fish and protein shakes, and bloggers encouraging us all to "just eat Real Food." When I signed on to be a mother, I knew it would entail making tough decisions, protecting my children and keeping them healthy as they grew and developed. I assumed that they would thrive and flourish, and I still think they will, but at this point I suspect it will be in spite of the Great Industrial Food Production Machine, not because of it.

Food is big business in the United States as it is everywhere in the world. Most of our celebrations and gatherings are centred around food (Thanksgiving dinner, Halloween parties, Passover), and that's not wrong, but it is hard to avoid. Nobody wants to be the obnoxious guest who, upon being invited for Easter dinner, tells the host that he or she can't eat anything with wheat or gluten in it, and that they really try to avoid dairy with growth hormones and grapes because grapes are part of the "dirty dozen," products grown with a significant amounts of pesticides.

I have friends whose kids struggle with obsessive-compulsive disorder or autism or sensory processing issues and many of them have tried ketogenic diets or anti-inflammatory diets, some with great results. But it's exhausting and expensive and all-consuming to think about the food that you're feeding your kid each and every day, all day long. I am lucky enough to be able to afford organic, gluten-free foods. I am inordinately lucky to have the time and the education to research what is healthiest for my kids, and I feel lucky that I love to cook. But I don't often feel confident that what I think I know today will be true tomorrow after someone else does a longitudinal study or some new research comes out. I often look around at other families who are much more casual about their meals and wonder if this is all for naught. Would my kids be just as healthy and productive and happy if their school lunches featured Hot Cheetos and Dr. Pepper a few times a week? Am I obsessing about this a little too much? Ultimately, the problem is that I don't know and I would rather err on the side of caution.

I wish that I could trust the Food and Drug Administration to police the food supply and that seed companies were more concerned about the health of their consumers than the money they're extorting from farmers. I wish that I didn't feel as if I needed a degree in biochemistry to determine what to feed my children. With all of the knowledge we have about how our diet affects our health, it seems absurd that unhealthy foods are cheaper and more readily available than fresh produce and organic meat. To quote a saying that popped up in my Facebook feed today, "Once upon a time, all food was organic." Unfortunately, food-as-business has replaced food-as-sustenance with companies such as Tyson and Monsanto putting their financial interests above all, using advertising tactics to convince consumers that their products are safe, and spending millions of dollars lobbying lawmakers to prevent labelling laws. As a mother, this hits me in the spot where I am most vulnerable.

We live in a culture where mothers are held almost solely responsible for both their children's safety and who their children are. If I had a nickel for every study that looked at what a mother ate when she was pregnant and related it to the child's brain development or birth weight or behaviour, I would be a rich woman. As mothers, we are set up to feel as though what we eat and, subsequently what we feed our children, is of paramount importance, yet wading through the stacks of conflicting information to determine what is healthy by this week's standards is daunting to say the least. As a college-educated, middle-class, mostly stay-at-home mother, I have the luxury of time and resources to spend researching food and preparing it. I don't live in a neighbourhood that is known as a "food desert," a common American term for areas where the only options for buying food are convenience stores stocked with cheap, canned food and snacks. I have access to fresh produce and meats within walking distance of my house. Although I do make choices about how much to budget for our family's food,

I am lucky enough to be able to afford the extra cost of mostly organic, completely gluten-free items and the trips to the naturopath who first diagnosed us. I often wonder about families with food allergies who visit food banks or buy the majority of their grocery items in stores that don't carry specialty items and who suffer the physical consequences of not being able to afford the things that they need the most. I am grateful every day that I have the time to cook most of our family's food from scratch because I remember my mother's struggle to feed hungry, growing kids on a limited budget after putting in a full day of work outside the home. Had it been an option, she would have loved to cook her signature dishes for us every night and pack meat loaf sandwiches for our school lunches. When money is scarce, choices become more about survival than long-term health, whether the families know the latest research or not. The repeated cuts to food stamp program (known as SNAP) and the restrictions placed on which items can be purchased with the vouchers have led to a record number of families seeking assistance from food banks and other sources. And although there is no shortage of judgment around how mothers feed their children, there is very little support for most mothers when it comes to doing just that. Meal preparation is largely considered women's work and it isn't relegated to the time one spends in the kitchen. As an uncompensated task that requires both set up and clean up, it is incredibly tempting for a busy mother to turn to convenience foods to feed her family rather than embarking on yet another full-time job—the job of meal preparation. My family is lucky to be in a position to stock our pantry with foods that won't make us sick and to choose whether or not to cook on any given day.

Because my kids won't get an education about food anywhere else, we talk about it a lot in our household. My girls are growing up highly aware of what they eat and are often willing to try foods that I never knew existed when I was their age. They see me cook nearly every day, and I emphasize the rule of "everything in moderation," which means that our freezer contains ice cream and chocolate chip cookie dough. When someone is craving jicama or corn on the cob and we can't find organic, it won't kill us to have conventionally grown produce.

In a way, I am grateful for our gluten intolerance because it has opened up an entirely new way of looking at our lives and our health. Although my husband is able to eat gluten without any problems, he is a terrific cook and takes some of the pressure off me by preparing the main meals on weekends and he is very careful to make sure it's all gluten free. Erin went through a phase where she baked cupcakes every weekend, and she has perfected a gluten-free sugar cookie that she gives as holiday gifts. Lauren often helps me make bread and loves chopping vegetables for salads, and I no longer worry about sending them to a friend's house or out to dinner without me because they are both aware of what they can and can't have. We talk about protein, carbohydrates, fibre and how much sugar is too much. We are all vigilant label readers and have seen first-hand how what we eat affects the way our bodies perform.

I do sometimes wonder what will happen when my girls move out on their own. Having spent their childhood watching my careful attitude toward food preparation and consumption, will they go crazy and eat french fries and drink Diet Coke all day just because I am no longer lecturing them about the horrible effects of aspartame? As they grow up, I do my best to not dictate their food choices and instead encourage them to connect the dots between what they eat and how they feel. If Erin cheats and eats some gluten at a pizza party with her girlfriends, I ask whether she thinks that the migraine she gets later that night is related. Does a sugar binge on a sleepover result in a sluggish day where Lauren just can't get going? If they are encouraged to be mindful and deliberate about what they put into their bodies, I believe the ultimate effect will be a positive one. I hope that the message they are getting from me is that it is important to know what you're eating and it's equally important to pay attention to how it makes you feel.

9.
My Mother Did Not Cook

DOMINIQUE O'NEILL

MY MOTHER DID NOT KNOW HOW TO COOK and she refused to learn. We lived in France, and when she was a girl, before the Second World War, her family had had servants. The war took them away, along with her family's wealth, and my mother never forgave the world for having robbed her of their services. They were her due.

She didn't burn water—she just forgot it until it evaporated while she stood by the stove lost in a book, then burned her hand removing the pan from the flame and cried. Milk boiled over and canned food stuck to the bottom of the pan and turned black.

Children know from a very young age what mothers are supposed to be and do, and if theirs meets expectations. Mine did not meet any: she worked and was shamefully divorced at a time when respectable women, even battered ones like her, stayed married and at home. Strange men came and waited by our door to see if she would receive them. That she never did could not redeem her reputation. She was excommunicated, said the priests, and neither she nor her children would gain entry into Heaven, no matter how virtuously they lived. We had to lie and say that our father was dead to even be allowed to go to Catholic school.

Walking home alone from my convent school, I used to try to catch glimpses of women at traditional tasks: sweeping their stoop while awaiting their own children, dusting their front room, or weeding their flowerbeds. A latchkey kid, I envied children whose mothers stayed at home, often invisibly—their presence and activity only betrayed by the smell of cooking wafting from their kitchens. I used to dream of a mother who had no face but wore an apron. The father figure carried a briefcase, but he was just an absence anyway.

My mother was an artist, with a Beaux-Arts diploma from a large city, which made her even more suspect to the small burg in which we lived, and its even smaller-minded burghers. She painted landscapes in oils on Sunday, always in order to sell them for extra cash or to barter with the butcher. Since oils are slow to dry, and her easel was set up in the middle of our small kitchen while she painted, and stashed in the bathroom between the shower and sink afterward, if I walked too close, I would collect slashes of brown, green, or blue, on the skirt and sleeves of my white and navy schoolgirl uniform. They were symbolic of my mother's "misfitedness"—they branded and shamed me—but I wore them with a silent stoicism worthy of a Saint Sebastian painting. I would not explain, even when other girls made remarks about them.

After we ran away from my father's house, she worked at whatever jobs she could find: delivering flyers on her bicycle and selling cheese at the market, teaching art and English in exchange for our keep as semi-boarders at the Catholic school. In those days, as she let us out the front door on our way to school in the morning, she would often say warningly: "*Je ne sais pas ce qu'il y aura à manger ce soir.*" (I don't know what there will be to eat tonight.) My sister and I lived with that fear all day; it gnawed at our stomachs, even as we swallowed the daily ration of boiled beans (the local crop) that was our lunch at the convent school. Yet I do not remember ever going to bed without the bowl of warm milk and soaked bread that constituted our normal dinner. It took me years to realize that, while the threat of hunger had crushed us, it had excited her, had made the day an adventure, a challenge to her own ingenuity. And she did find ways to earn quick money: drawing posters for merchants, decorating their shop windows, selling pyrographed and painted wooden boxes to tourists, or running errands on her bicycle. Eventually, she was hired as an X-ray technician and life stabilized a bit. She worked a twelve-hour day then, five and a half days a week, with two hours off for lunch—a normal workload in France in those days.

But meals were simply too great a demand on her strength, time, and patience. They were crisis points. Dinner was a late and exhausted disaster of snappy words, with full fights on weekends. She and my older sister argued a lot, and our kitchen table was their favourite battleground. Since my mother was prone to tantrums, she threw any object that came to hand—and would shatter satisfyingly—across the kitchen, because that's what artists do during passionate fits. They can't help themselves. Life was simply too much. She deserved better. Our father, she would say to excuse herself afterward, had broken so many plates that, by the end, she had bought plastic ones that just bounced off the walls. So it wasn't the burned food, it was the anger that spiked it that made it indigestible. As I wasn't allowed to bring my book to the table, I retreated into myself and tried to shut them out.

But meals aren't only about the need to eat: they are also a time for togetherness, and, as such, can be an occasion to express and receive love. Even the simplest ones around a cereal box can celebrate togetherness and sharing. Regardless of whether they happen in morning haste or seemingly mundane end-of-the-day chatter, meals offer an opportunity for bonding as hands reach out and pass bowls, plates, and dishes filled with warmth and smells that anticipate taste.

We knew this, my sister and I, because we had a great-grandmother with whom we spent the holidays. Mémé knew how to cook and still made the traditional dishes she had learned as a girl. She took great pride in her cooking, especially in the sacrosanct *pot-au-feu* (beef marrow and oxtail soup) that simmered all day on the back of her coal-heated stove, its heavenly aroma promising later delights. Sundays smelled of church incense in the morning and of *pot-au-feu* for the rest of the day.

Mémé made the humblest meal into a feast, even when there was little to eat. If our dinner consisted of a soft-boiled egg, it wasn't merely some nondescript egg from the grocery store. It was an egg laid that very morning by the landlady's best layer, in our courtyard's own henhouse, and brought over, still warm, with a bit of straw and a feather attached to its shell to attest to its authenticity. Madame Prieur, the landlady, had brought three eggs in a little basket when she had heard we would be visiting, because she knew that Mémé would only give us the best, and the very best was this beautiful and perfect egg, now proudly standing in one of Mémé's hand-painted porcelain eggcups, awaiting the delicate dunking of thin strips of country bread.

Simple cooking became a grand ceremony: if we had been very good, she dissolved a few spoonfuls of sugar in a little vinegar in a small pan over the stove and we watched in amazement as the pale liquid magically became golden bubbles that turned into thick caramel, then hardened into candy as it cooled. On special days, she made a *tôt-fait,* a Yorkshire pudding served as a dessert that ballooned marvellously in the oven but quickly deflated when taken out, like a *mongolfière* that has just landed. And in the evening, she often ate an apple and would peel it in a single unbroken ribbon directly above the stove so that it fell and lay on the hot surface, drying slowly, while we played *petits chevaux* (parcheesi) under the lamp. It curled and shrank, releasing the wonderful smell of roasted apple into her small cottage—and into our dreams.

Imagine this: two apron-clad little girls stand on either side of a tall white-haired woman in black, like altar boys on either side of the celebrant, and watch the miracle of food preparation in awed silence, each step a tangible and paced ritual.

Our own role was limited to setting the table. *"Mettez la table!"* Mémé would say when all was nearly ready, and we would run into the dark and cold dining room and raid it, quickly pulling dishes from the belly of the majestic carved buffet—a relic from those past days of grandeur—and fleeing back to the safety of the lit and warm kitchen, to the humble table with its traditional oilcloth on which we disposed our loot: forks and napkins on the left, spoons and knives on the right of the soup plates.

These rituals and dishes are my precious "Proustian madeleine" memory markers: they anchor not only a taste and an odour but something more nebulously yet essential—the notion of what "home" might mean: a mood, an intimacy, a feeling of peace, of belonging, of acceptance.

Sadly however, the stereotype of mothers who bake love as the ultimate sweet to serve to their family is so universal that those of us who did not have such a mother are not only silenced but also secretly ashamed of not having deserved one. I must admit that

I once spent a very liberating evening with people who had bad mothers. It was an accidental discovery. We were sitting on the terrace of my sister's beach house in France, sipping good wine and enjoying a perfect meal fresh from the sea, when she mentioned that the mother of one of the guests had passed away during the winter, so we offered polite condolences. "I hated her," the guest replied, "not as a person, but as a failed nurturer—and now I hate her for taking all of her secrets with her when she died. She was so selfish!" For a moment, we were stunned by her shocking admission. Then stories (s)tumbled out. Once we began sharing memories, however, it was such a relief to speak openly about women for whom motherhood had been a burden, about their anger, and how it had been channeled into constant criticism of their children. We were never—and never would be—good enough to deserve their love. Regardless of what we had made of our lives, of how successful we might have become, we had never gotten over it.

But the only way to redeem oneself and to undo at least some of the pain—the only possible revenge in fact—is to become the mother one wanted to have. (I do say, rather flippantly, that it has been easy for me to be a good mother: I just ask myself what my own would have done and do the opposite.) Inspired by our memories of Mémé, my sister and I became loving cooks. She is forever feeding friends and relatives, a cheese-loving poodle and three contented cats and I, as a young bride new to Canada, pored over French cookbooks to become worthy of my heritage, and then, as a mother of my own two apron-clad little girls, raised them on "homemade" everything, even croissants that took all day to make. They baked with me as soon as they were old enough to stand on a chair, and are better at it than I am because not only did they watch and participate, but they also learned intuitively, as only children can. Their recipes, I like to think, echo with pleasant childhood memories. For them, kitchens are a place for giggles and confidences, and advice passed on, along with stories dotted with "Do you remember when?"

Still, I spent years trying too hard and would become upset when things did not turn out perfectly. I didn't learn my lesson until our youngest served a meal she was unhappy with and brought such a cloud of negativity to the table that I said: "I'd much rather eat a bad dinner than have to come to the table angry and disappointed." As soon as the words were out of my mouth, I realized that this was what I had been doing all these years. The silence that followed confirmed it. I can only wish that I had realized it much sooner.

My husband did not cook as a boy, although he is the eldest of eight children and had to do his share of household tasks. His mum—who is a loving and sincere mother and fondly recalls how his father bought her a cookbook as a wedding present—was solely in charge of their meals. By the time we married, however, cooking was no longer a woman's exclusive duty, and he joined me in the kitchen, baked our bread, cooked our fish and meat, and is famous for his biscuits, gingerbread, and fries. Food planning, shopping, and preparation were, and still are, shared. It is part of our "together-time," a prelude to our daily candlelit dinners. As our girls became teens, everyone planned and cooked one or two meals per week as a chef and then helped someone else the next night as a sous-chef. And when the grandchildren arrived, we welcomed them into our kitchen for hot lunch preparation, cookie making, and cake decorating for holidays and birthdays.

But girls belong in the kitchen by tradition, so mine slipped in easily, as did my two granddaughters, one for whom the making of blueberry muffins for breakfast when we visit has been our special ritual since she was small. I didn't raise boys, and even though more men cook today, boys are still "benevolently" marginalized in that they are not *expected* to cook and so are not necessarily included. Boys only visit the kitchen to open the fridge, right? "Well," explained my eldest grandson, then aged ten, big eyes round and innocent, hands spread out helplessly in front of him, "I'm just not *into* it, Mamy!" "But you are *into* eating" I replied rather shortly, "so you should contribute. If you won't cook, then you must clean!" He pointed out virtuously that he does empty the dishwasher and set the table, but when faced with scrubbing pots, he agreed to try cooking. We made French toast together the next morning, and he stood the slices of baguette on end to make sure that they cooked in the middle, a novel approach that gave him the key to good cooking: handle and feel the food as a living entity, and give it your whole attention and respect. You have to nurture it before you can nurture those you love with it.

My youngest grandson, aged nine, had words of wisdom for me while he was making his special shrimp dish: "I'll tell you a secret, Mamy. Garlic gets bitter if you overbrown it, so you have to be patient and cook it slowly, then take it out of the pan while you cook the shrimp." He learned that from our friend Geoffrey-the-fiddler. Men and boys cooking together and learning to nurture others—such wonderful bonding, such hope for sharing household responsibilities, and such potential relief for overburdened women. Geoffrey told him another secret: It's even more pleasurable to watch other people eating the food you prepared than to eat it yourself—quite a lesson for a young boy.

Now that I am a grandmother, I am so very conscious of the fact that my time with the little ones will be inscribed in their childhood memories, as Mémé's is in mine, and I want them to remember that their Papy and I treasured them and cherished every moment we spent with them. Grandparenting, of course, is such a joy. No longer the primary caregivers—the ones who must combine full-time jobs, marriage, chauffeuring, errands, meals and cleaning, and somehow bring up a new generation of moral and sociable citizens—we enjoy our grandchildren's visits for the enormous pleasure of just being together. We don't do things *for* them but *with* them. We just try to offer opportunities and open doors to learning. Cooking with them is a privilege, and we feel blessed to guide their hands as they handle a knife, to stand beside them at the stove, to explain and show, and to clean up the inevitable spills. As we grow older, knowing how quickly time passes, we learn to live in the now, to treasure those moments, and to take mental snapshots of them: the boy standing at the stove, watching his French toast become golden or his shrimp turn from mushy grey to delicate coral pink, the girl at the counter sifting her muffin mixture with great concentration, and the little one, aged two, standing on a sturdy wooden chair to decorate her own birthday cake and calling out gleefully as her sprinkles drop to the floor: "I'm doing my cake, Mummy! I'm doing my cake!"

From one generation to the next and beyond, the message is the same: I am cooking with you because I want us to share this moment, because the care I give this food is a testament of my love for you.

10.
Fortress of Confection

Lessons from My Yankee Grandmother

ERICA CAVANAGH

EVEN NOW I SEE HER DRIVING, sitting up straight with both hands on the upper steering wheel, her chin lifted as she gazes at the road ahead. If she stops, it will only be to use the restroom. She considers buying food on the road wasteful, so she's packed a roast beef sandwich, saltines, and carrots in an old green metal cooler, and she'll stop in Herkimer, New York, about halfway between our houses, to eat in the Howard Johnson's parking lot.

When I was a girl, I'd look for her out my bedroom window. Grammy lived six hours away, so if she left at eight, she'd be here around two, but if she left at ten, the possibility of waiting for her until four seemed unbearable. Forlorn, I'd wander into my brother's room. "She'd better hurry up," he'd say. We couldn't wait to get our hands on her Swedish thumb cookies, those buttery shortbread pillows filled with frosting and sprinkles. She was the only person in the world who made them. They were her signature. They were how we knew that Grammy was Grammy, and that we were hers and she was ours. Her presence even caused our parents to behave better. All afternoon we trained our ears on the front door for the moment when we'd hear her knocking snow off of her boot heels against the stoop, and we would go flying down the stairs, not to throw our arms around her—Grammy would not be mauled—no, we halted before her in our tracks, ready for appraisal. Grammy laughed. "Well, how's my Jim? And how's my Erica?" We were bashful little gremlins eager for the cookie tins. The cookie tins! Where were the cookie tins? We would never be so demanding out loud, although we could barely contain ourselves from hurtling straight out to her car to hurry them in.

Five tins sat on the sideboard like Pandora's boxes, and all I wanted to do was pry the lids off, my whole body wound up as I waited for a signal from the adults that we could open them. Those tins held our fates. You could never be sure what Grammy would bring. At least two would contain Swedish thumb cookies, and if I crossed my fingers hard, maybe one would be fudge crumble bars, and another cherry coconut bars, layered in maraschino cherries and coconut shavings like a confectionary incarnation of the *White Christmas* movie. But beware the wild card, like the time Grammy brought an iffy-looking interloper with a brown jammy layer. Date bars, she called them. I peered at said bars suspiciously. They looked healthy. I was seven or eight and had never tried a date, but I was sure dates contained something sneaky that tricked you into thinking adult stuff was tasty like the prune juice Mom wanted us to drink: "To help your bowels," she'd say. I never touched it. As we waited for the signal, I was beginning to discover a modicum of pleasure in my restraint, as if it were some sign of my worth that I could exercise enough control to possibly achieve that very grown-up principle: *All good things come to those who wait.*

When we visited Grammy Taft in Monson, Massachusetts, the tins were arrayed on her kitchen counter, ready to be devoured. We could have one cookie at a time, maybe two, and we were to eat where we wouldn't leave crumbs. Grammy's house was like a museum. In one of the rooms, which she called "the parlour," there was a satiny Victorian sofa with a fractured wooden armrest. The broken arm troubled me; I wished I could have fixed it but didn't have the tools to do so. We never sat in the parlour, and we never entered through the front door but stepped through the breezeway and around the back into the homier living room. Whenever anyone entered or left, the leather strap of sleigh bells hanging from the door jingled. Grampa's galoshes used to be by the backdoor, too. I never knew him well, Bob Taft, but I remember his mottled hands and the pressure of sharing a table with him. If Jim or I hesitated to take one more bite of beans, he'd say: "Don't you want to be a part of The Clean Plate Club?" It made me think he'd grown up with few means, but then after his sister Margaret's death, a large

black-and-white photograph of a Victorian m
over the fireplace. Apparently, Grampa and his
grown up in that mansion with maids and a c
floors, and President Taft once visited them. No
about this before. The mansion had been known a
now it was a funeral home protected by the Nat
Historic Places. We don't talk about how my gra
lost its wealth. Mishandling of money, drinking
of 1929 have all been mentioned, reluctantly, li
thing that should be kept in a sealed envelope in
a secret crawlspace in the house.

But I liked to get inside of things and try to unde
came to be. When I was little and loved dolls, Gra
two antique ones that had been my mother's. It
to me that Mom had been a girl. There was a bl
Cinderella ball gown and a brunette in a baroque
golden fringe. From the moment I learned that Gr
had made the dresses, I was seized with pride ab
talents. How? Who taught her? And who mac
boxes? Running my finger over the studs on the n
scrutinized their innards. I peered into the crawl spe
beds and found boxes of glass-plate negatives, ther
on the carpet, and I very carefully slid the square
the light box to see who was in there. I thought ma
inscrutable faces of our ancestors or bland landsca
I wasn't sure what I was seeing: so many of the pho
of dead young men, their bodies blown back, conto
their uniforms torn.

I learned to like containment and feel safe in it. In
and brooches Grammy wore I began to see that el
a bulwark. She wore low heels, flats, and black l
Never sneakers, sweats, sweatshirts, or T-shirts. E
fed her chestnut bay, JayJay, his oats, Ruby Taft l
and robust as she wielded a pitchfork, cleaning mar
stable out back. She had the most impressive calves
from riding horseback. She stood like an athlete, str
planted and shoulders squared. She could be intim
had a way of narrowing her eyes on you, listening

could barely contain ourselves from hurtling straight out to her car to hurry them in.

Five tins sat on the sideboard like Pandora's boxes, and all I wanted to do was pry the lids off, my whole body wound up as I waited for a signal from the adults that we could open them. Those tins held our fates. You could never be sure what Grammy would bring. At least two would contain Swedish thumb cookies, and if I crossed my fingers hard, maybe one would be fudge crumble bars, and another cherry coconut bars, layered in maraschino cherries and coconut shavings like a confectionary incarnation of the *White Christmas* movie. But beware the wild card, like the time Grammy brought an iffy-looking interloper with a brown jammy layer. Date bars, she called them. I peered at said bars suspiciously. They looked healthy. I was seven or eight and had never tried a date, but I was sure dates contained something sneaky that tricked you into thinking adult stuff was tasty like the prune juice Mom wanted us to drink: "To help your bowels," she'd say. I never touched it. As we waited for the signal, I was beginning to discover a modicum of pleasure in my restraint, as if it were some sign of my worth that I could exercise enough control to possibly achieve that very grown-up principle: *All good things come to those who wait.*

When we visited Grammy Taft in Monson, Massachusetts, the tins were arrayed on her kitchen counter, ready to be devoured. We could have one cookie at a time, maybe two, and we were to eat where we wouldn't leave crumbs. Grammy's house was like a museum. In one of the rooms, which she called "the parlour," there was a satiny Victorian sofa with a fractured wooden armrest. The broken arm troubled me; I wished I could have fixed it but didn't have the tools to do so. We never sat in the parlour, and we never entered through the front door but stepped through the breezeway and around the back into the homier living room. Whenever anyone entered or left, the leather strap of sleigh bells hanging from the door jingled. Grampa's galoshes used to be by the backdoor, too. I never knew him well, Bob Taft, but I remember his mottled hands and the pressure of sharing a table with him. If Jim or I hesitated to take one more bite of beans, he'd say: "Don't you want to be a part of The Clean Plate Club?" It made me think he'd grown up with few means, but then after his sister Margaret's death, a large black-and-white photograph of a Victorian mansion was hung over the fireplace. Apparently, Grampa and his five siblings had grown up in that mansion with maids and a cook and multiple floors, and President Taft once visited them. No one had spoken about this before. The mansion had been known as "Hillside," and now it was a funeral home protected by the National Register of Historic Places. We don't talk about how my grandfather's family lost its wealth. Mishandling of money, drinking, and the Crash of 1929 have all been mentioned, reluctantly, like a scandalous thing that should be kept in a sealed envelope in a locked safe in a secret crawlspace in the house.

But I liked to get inside of things and try to understand how they came to be. When I was little and loved dolls, Grammy pulled out two antique ones that had been my mother's. It seemed curious to me that Mom had been a girl. There was a blonde wearing a Cinderella ball gown and a brunette in a baroque rosy one with a golden fringe. From the moment I learned that Grammy's mother had made the dresses, I was seized with pride about her artistic talents. How? Who taught her? And who made these music boxes? Running my finger over the studs on the metal cylinder, I scrutinized their innards. I peered into the crawl spaces behind the beds and found boxes of glass-plate negatives, then sprawled out on the carpet, and I very carefully slid the square glass plate into the light box to see who was in there. I thought maybe I'd see the inscrutable faces of our ancestors or bland landscapes, so at first I wasn't sure what I was seeing: so many of the photographs were of dead young men, their bodies blown back, contorted, and still, their uniforms torn.

I learned to like containment and feel safe in it. In the cardigans and brooches Grammy wore I began to see that elegance can be a bulwark. She wore low heels, flats, and black leather boots. Never sneakers, sweats, sweatshirts, or T-shirts. Even when she fed her chestnut bay, JayJay, his oats, Ruby Taft looked stately and robust as she wielded a pitchfork, cleaning manure from his stable out back. She had the most impressive calves, sturdy ones from riding horseback. She stood like an athlete, straight up, feet planted and shoulders squared. She could be intimidating. She had a way of narrowing her eyes on you, listening as she made

I once spent a very liberating evening with people who had bad mothers. It was an accidental discovery. We were sitting on the terrace of my sister's beach house in France, sipping good wine and enjoying a perfect meal fresh from the sea, when she mentioned that the mother of one of the guests had passed away during the winter, so we offered polite condolences. "I hated her," the guest replied, "not as a person, but as a failed nurturer—and now I hate her for taking all of her secrets with her when she died. She was so selfish!" For a moment, we were stunned by her shocking admission. Then stories (s)tumbled out. Once we began sharing memories, however, it was such a relief to speak openly about women for whom motherhood had been a burden, about their anger, and how it had been channeled into constant criticism of their children. We were never—and never would be—good enough to deserve their love. Regardless of what we had made of our lives, of how successful we might have become, we had never gotten over it.

But the only way to redeem oneself and to undo at least some of the pain—the only possible revenge in fact—is to become the mother one wanted to have. (I do say, rather flippantly, that it has been easy for me to be a good mother: I just ask myself what my own would have done and do the opposite.) Inspired by our memories of Mémé, my sister and I became loving cooks. She is forever feeding friends and relatives, a cheese-loving poodle and three contented cats and I, as a young bride new to Canada, pored over French cookbooks to become worthy of my heritage, and then, as a mother of my own two apron-clad little girls, raised them on "homemade" everything, even croissants that took all day to make. They baked with me as soon as they were old enough to stand on a chair, and are better at it than I am because not only did they watch and participate, but they also learned intuitively, as only children can. Their recipes, I like to think, echo with pleasant childhood memories. For them, kitchens are a place for giggles and confidences, and advice passed on, along with stories dotted with "Do you remember when?"

Still, I spent years trying too hard and would become upset when things did not turn out perfectly. I didn't learn my lesson until our youngest served a meal she was unhappy with and brought such a cloud of negativity to the table that I said: "I'd much rather eat a bad dinner than have to come to the table angry and disappointed." As soon as the words were out of my mouth, I realized that this was what I had been doing all these years. The silence that followed confirmed it. I can only wish that I had realized it much sooner.

My husband did not cook as a boy, although he is the eldest of eight children and had to do his share of household tasks. His mum—who is a loving and sincere mother and fondly recalls how his father bought her a cookbook as a wedding present—was solely in charge of their meals. By the time we married, however, cooking was no longer a woman's exclusive duty, and he joined me in the kitchen, baked our bread, cooked our fish and meat, and is famous for his biscuits, gingerbread, and fries. Food planning, shopping, and preparation were, and still are, shared. It is part of our "together-time," a prelude to our daily candlelit dinners. As our girls became teens, everyone planned and cooked one or two meals per week as a chef and then helped someone else the next night as a sous-chef. And when the grandchildren arrived, we welcomed them into our kitchen for hot lunch preparation, cookie making, and cake decorating for holidays and birthdays.

But girls belong in the kitchen by tradition, so mine slipped in easily, as did my two granddaughters, one for whom the making of blueberry muffins for breakfast when we visit has been our special ritual since she was small. I didn't raise boys, and even though more men cook today, boys are still "benevolently" marginalized in that they are not *expected* to cook and so are not necessarily included. Boys only visit the kitchen to open the fridge, right? "Well," explained my eldest grandson, then aged ten, big eyes round and innocent, hands spread out helplessly in front of him, "I'm just not *into* it, Mamy!" "But you are *into* eating" I replied rather shortly, "so you should contribute. If you won't cook, then you must clean!" He pointed out virtuously that he does empty the dishwasher and set the table, but when faced with scrubbing pots, he agreed to try cooking. We made French toast together the next morning, and he stood the slices of baguette on end to make sure that they cooked in the middle, a novel approach that gave him the key to good cooking: handle and feel the food as a living entity, and give it your whole attention and respect. You have to nurture it before you can nurture those you love with it.

My youngest grandson, aged nine, had words of wisdom for me while he was making his special shrimp dish: "I'll tell you a secret, Mamy. Garlic gets bitter if you overbrown it, so you have to be patient and cook it slowly, then take it out of the pan while you cook the shrimp." He learned that from our friend Geoffrey-the-fiddler. Men and boys cooking together and learning to nurture others—such wonderful bonding, such hope for sharing household responsibilities, and such potential relief for overburdened women. Geoffrey told him another secret: It's even more pleasurable to watch other people eating the food you prepared than to eat it yourself—quite a lesson for a young boy.

Now that I am a grandmother, I am so very conscious of the fact that my time with the little ones will be inscribed in their childhood memories, as Mémé's is in mine, and I want them to remember that their Papy and I treasured them and cherished every moment we spent with them. Grandparenting, of course, is such a joy. No longer the primary caregivers—the ones who must combine full-time jobs, marriage, chauffeuring, errands, meals and cleaning, and somehow bring up a new generation of moral and sociable citizens—we enjoy our grandchildren's visits for the enormous pleasure of just being together. We don't do things *for* them but *with* them. We just try to offer opportunities and open doors to learning. Cooking with them is a privilege, and we feel blessed to guide their hands as they handle a knife, to stand beside them at the stove, to explain and show, and to clean up the inevitable spills. As we grow older, knowing how quickly time passes, we learn to live in the now, to treasure those moments, and to take mental snapshots of them: the boy standing at the stove, watching his French toast become golden or his shrimp turn from mushy grey to delicate coral pink, the girl at the counter sifting her muffin mixture with great concentration, and the little one, aged two, standing on a sturdy wooden chair to decorate her own birthday cake and calling out gleefully as her sprinkles drop to the floor: "I'm doing my cake, Mummy! I'm doing my cake!"

From one generation to the next and beyond, the message is the same: I am cooking with you because I want us to share this moment, because the care I give this food is a testament of my love for you.

10.
Fortress of Confection

Lessons from My Yankee Grandmother

ERICA CAVANAGH

EVEN NOW I SEE HER DRIVING, sitting up straight with both hands on the upper steering wheel, her chin lifted as she gazes at the road ahead. If she stops, it will only be to use the restroom. She considers buying food on the road wasteful, so she's packed a roast beef sandwich, saltines, and carrots in an old green metal cooler, and she'll stop in Herkimer, New York, about halfway between our houses, to eat in the Howard Johnson's parking lot.

When I was a girl, I'd look for her out my bedroom window. Grammy lived six hours away, so if she left at eight, she'd be here around two, but if she left at ten, the possibility of waiting for her until four seemed unbearable. Forlorn, I'd wander into my brother's room. "She'd better hurry up," he'd say. We couldn't wait to get our hands on her Swedish thumb cookies, those buttery shortbread pillows filled with frosting and sprinkles. She was the only person in the world who made them. They were her signature. They were how we knew that Grammy was Grammy, and that we were hers and she was ours. Her presence even caused our parents to behave better. All afternoon we trained our ears on the front door for the moment when we'd hear her knocking snow off of her boot heels against the stoop, and we would go flying down the stairs, not to throw our arms around her—Grammy would not be mauled—no, we halted before her in our tracks, ready for appraisal. Grammy laughed. "Well, how's my Jim? And how's my Erica?" We were bashful little gremlins eager for the cookie tins. The cookie tins! Where were the cookie tins? We would never be so demanding out loud, although we calculated judgments. If she suspected you of something, even if you hadn't done anything, she'd tell you that you had. You'd put the dishes away in the wrong place on purpose; you'd let your knives go dull, as my mother had and got a scolding: "If you're not going to use the sharpening stone I gave you, I'm taking it back where it will be *used*."

When I was a girl, my mother sometimes cried to me that her mother didn't love her. I didn't know what to say, but I sensed that love was fragile and favour lost with a mood shift as when a child didn't anticipate exactly what a parent wanted and obey. I felt braced around Grammy, not coddled. I tried not to incite her scowl, but I was a curious and wilful girl who sometimes didn't come when Grammy called but lingered in her yard waiting for the deer and the foxes to come out of the forest. In Grammy's eyes, my independence was an affront and an inspiration. She loved the company of young people; she showed great interest in them, especially in the years when they were making decisions about their schooling, their work, and their future families. She welcomed her grandchildren's friends with lamb stew, sweets, and her generous, genuine attention. Not until I was a woman could I see that Grammy didn't want to be dependent on anyone or perceived as feeble in any capacity. She wanted people to depend on her, and she wanted to depend on herself too. She would not be cowed into staying home just because of a little heavy snow. She would dig her way out and drive herself down to the butcher's in Palmer, get her flank steak, and have a sharp knife on hand to slice it properly.

About being a young lady born at the beginning of the twentieth century, the actress Fay Wray said, "Deportment was more important than soul-searching." The quote reminds me of my grandmother, born in 1913. She was so well mannered that I knew little about her. In 1992, when I was a freshman in college, I took black-and-white photographs of her for a photojournalism project. In the last of the series, she's sitting in my mother's living room. We must have just finished Thanksgiving dinner, and she's sitting alone on the couch, not looking at the camera; she's not quite comfortable with me training my lens on her. Loosely, she holds an empty dessert plate on her lap, the fork idle, her other elbow propped on the back of the couch, her head not quite resting against her curled hand but still upright as she gazes resignedly at something outside the frame. The long corridor of her life seemed to be there in that look, many of the people who once populated it now gone. She'd been a widow six years by then. Her husband had died on a New Year's Eve. The funeral took place on an overcast day, not so cold, but slushy. The service was held in his childhood home in the tall, wood paneled room that had once been the family library. During his daughters' eulogies, I kept thinking *the children probably weren't allowed in here*; I kept expecting to hear them running up and down the stairs. Now the home was a business for the dead. All that could slip through the hands was all too clear. Maybe that's why Grammy refused to be driven to his burial. She drove herself. She was seventy-three. I sat beside her in the front seat, a memory that seems off to me because she favoured my brother, so in this memory I keep thinking he should have been the one up there with her, the captain's mate with the captain. It couldn't have been me. But I remember her hands on the steering wheel, steadied at ten and two o'clock; and I remember her eyes staring vaguely ahead, the abstracted look on her face. I was twelve, and although it was only my second funeral, I kept thinking I should know what to do or say, that there must be some wise gesture that would somehow account for the gravity of losing her husband. But when I thought about uttering anything, it seemed so wrong that I became afraid of my voice. That if I uttered a single word it would tear at some sacred pact about dignity, about speaking out of turn, about being respectful. So I tried to imitate her composure. Hands folded in my lap, I tried to gaze out the window as she did, although I kept stealing glances at the side of her face, wondering if she would cry. I was always looking at her to see what I was and was not allowed to do.

My grandmother thrived after her husband's death. Privately, I would remark on this to myself whenever I would notice the brightness of her skin, her gusto, her chuckle, how good she looked in a cardigan now that her shoulders appeared less heavy. I told no one because it didn't seem prudent to notice such a thing, how happy she seemed, how self-sufficient, how much better she looked in her later seventies and eighties than she had in her sixties.

By the time I started working in Benin, West Africa, I could attribute my plucky, independent spirit to my grandmother. I'd been living there a year when I came home for a month's visit and drove out to see her. When she answered the door, "Well," she said, smiling, then dramatically threw her head back, clasping her hand to her heart: "Thank goodness you haven't been trampled by the elephants!" She loved to get on the road, so we drove to a restaurant on top of a hill near South Hadley, where her parents used to take her for ice cream. A brisk and bright day, she wore a pressed ivory rain jacket over a light yellow sweater, and as the wind fluffed her cap of silver hair, I was thinking how lovely she was. We did not go in to eat anything; we just wanted the view. Eyes squinting, looking down on the valley of autumn leaves, she asked me, "What is it about Africa?" She'd had a girlfriend who moved there and didn't want to come back. I couldn't say what kept her girlfriend there and couldn't know then how much that place would become a part of my ear. When I offered to take the wheel for the drive back to Monson, I was surprised she acquiesced. By way of excuse (though she didn't need one), she said she'd raked her entire yard the day before. "It wore your poor grandmother out!" She was eighty-five, and somewhere on the road between Chicopee and Monson, Ruby Taft, born Ruby Mae Churchill, started telling me things for the first time, totally unexpected things about her marriage, something she had never discussed with me before. Perhaps I'd told her I wasn't sure I'd get married. She told me I had to be careful about whom I chose. I assumed she said so because both her daughters' marriages had ended. Instead she told me that in the first years of her marriage, when she and Grampa lived in Richmond, Virginia, he forbade her from going out. It was the first time she'd lived away from her home state, and she had no way of making friends. She said Grampa had the idea that women weren't to be trusted, and that he'd gotten this idea from a man who used to take him fishing, a Mr. Whitney, she said pointedly, the father of one of his Yale buddies. There was tightness and determination in her voice as she recounted a time she'd been to his home for dinner and witnessed how he put down his wife in front of the company.

113

"Love at first sight," I remembered Grampa saying when I'd asked him once about meeting Grammy. They'd met at a garden party and married in 1938 when she was twenty-five and he a year older, and soon after moved to Richmond for Grampa's work. She'd never experienced such humidity. "I'd hang sheets out to dry in the morning, and they'd still be wet at night," Grammy said with laugh. It wasn't the whole time they lived there that her husband didn't want her going out. "About a year," she recalled. She never felt comfortable in the South. If she was walking along a sidewalk and a black man was walking towards her, rather than sharing the sidewalk when they passed each other, from a long way off, he'd step off into the gutter. She looked vaguely at the floor, her brow wrinkling. "You felt it wasn't right," she said. With the birth of her first child, her steely will shot right back up her spine, and she fled back to Massachusetts where she moved right next door to her parents. Her husband soon followed.

That same year, in 1942, M. F. K. Fisher published *How to Cook a Wolf,* a charming and didactic memoir of recipes instructing home cooks on how to stretch ingredients during the WWII food shortages and still maintain a sense of humour and dignity. Having grown up under the New England adage, "Eat it up, wear it out, make it do, or do without," my grandmother likely needed no instruction on frugality. She indulged in making sweets from scratch—her own mother had been the same way—but when it came to coupon clipping and looking for a good deal in the paper, Grammy was a Yankee. I doubt she read M. F. K. Fisher. She didn't read literature, but she watched the nightly news and read *The Springfield Republican* daily. She possessed a whole arsenal of recipes her mother had clipped from their pages and passed on to her when she got married. My grandmother had her own wolves to keep back: her mercurial moods, her occasional paranoia, her fear of losing a child to germs or undertow or sick strangers. She'd lost her own baby brother to meningitis. She was fiercely protective. When we were small, she'd follow my brother and me into public bathroom stalls and lay toilet paper down on the seat. She could shun her own like a queen, too, without apology. To admit her own flaws fell beneath her pride, so I was surprised when, after Grammy died, my mother found among Grammy's papers a

Dear Abby letter from a mother living in the 1950s who's terribly remorseful for taking her anger out on her children. She calls them "innocent little dears." It made me wonder if some part of her knew an object of anger is often a bystander. Thinking about Grammy's experience of marriage, I wondered if she'd built a kind of fortress and sanctuary by shoring up her mother's recipes and in that place could feel confident and create what she wanted to create so well and so generously.

Not long before my brother got married, I wanted to put together an heirloom recipe book for his fiancée, so I asked my grandmother not to give me her usual twenty-five dollar check for Christmas but to write out her recipes. Her hand was getting shakier, and I sensed that soon she might stop writing all together. That Christmas, she gave me nine recipes, and all but one was for dessert: fudge crumble bars, cherry coconut bars, Swedish thumb cookies, marshmallow fudge cakes, blonde brownies, all written in slanted cursive. She'd noted their origins at the top of each lined index card; most had come from her mother, Ada, "Great-grandmother Churchill." When I was a girl, the fudge crumble bars had been my favourites, but it seemed impossible to say which were my favourites now. I just loved my grandmother's handwriting and the details particular to her, as in where she wrote, "1/2 cup shortening – We use butter." The words are a trace of who she was.

I even liked the date bars now. According to Grammy's shaky blue-ink script, they did not come from her mother but from the "Mass Mutual Ins. Co. Kitchen." When I asked her how she got a recipe from an insurance company, she said she'd worked there. When she graduated from high school, she took a job at the branch in Springfield and loved having her own money. Going down to the lunch counter and having lunch in the little cafeteria seemed exotic. Having a change purse with cash she could spend on herself made her feel giddy and grown up. They put the confections right by the cash register where you couldn't resist them. She loved the date bars, so she asked the girls at the lunch counter for the recipe. When I asked why she didn't go on working there, her brows knit; she paused, as though checking in with what she might say. Her parents were headed to Florida one summer, and they didn't want her to be home alone, unchaperoned, so she had to quit her job and join them. She was twenty or twenty-one. She couldn't remember what age exactly, only that she started courting thereafter.

When I was younger, I thought you had choices, and the right choices allowed the world to open up and up like a widening corridor. Only if you made the wrong choices did the world narrow and close. There were circumstances one couldn't control like a debilitating illness or an injury or the daunting mountain of poverty, but I thought that for someone like me who grew up in a suburb and graduated from college with manageable debt, the rest was relatively open, if you worked hard, that is, and took nothing for granted. Pursue what you love, share what you have with others, and be really discerning about not choosing the wrong marriage—that's what would lead to a fulfilling life—yet my simple formula didn't quite pan out. There is too much we cannot and do not know about our own behaviour or the behaviour of others, and how it will all unfold. Still, I am fortunate. I was born in a place and time when sane persons do not object to girls pursuing their studies, whereas in my grandmother's era, few women went to college and far fewer were encouraged to do so. She was expected to get married, and that's how she would be supported. But there had been a time, a chance, when Ruby had worked, when she had looked forward to the money in her pocket and the date bars at the end of the line.

When my grandmother could no longer live on her own, she moved to an assisted living facility in Rochester, New York, my hometown, about five miles from my mother. I lived in Virginia by then, and that Christmas when I visited her tiny beige apartment, Grammy was in the bathroom and had called me to come in so I could help her pull up her pants. "I have no shame anymore," she said. She was ninety-six. Her legs had gotten so skinny, and her feet were terribly swollen from sitting all the time. "Grammy, would you like to put your feet up?" I asked. Yes, she would, she nodded, so I pulled out a chair and helped her lift her heels. We chatted, or rather, I shouted as she held her hands up to her ears as if that could amplify the sound. She'd been doing this elephant-ear thing for years. She simply refused to wear hearing aids. She said they didn't work. She'd never even tried one, but she'd heard the reports. There was no convincing her otherwise, and that seemed just. Grammy needed help with so many things now—cooking, dressing, cutting her nails—and although her voice had become diminutive, like a well-behaved child's, I felt happy that she could still exercise certain refusals. Not until I was back in Virginia did I realize that we'd had no fudge crumble bars, no Swedish thumb cookies, no cookie tins at all that Christmas or on any other visit for several years.

All our lives, Grammy Taft had expressed her love for us in two main ways: she baked and drove hundreds of miles to see us, and now she could do neither. When this dawned on me, the earth seemed to open up like a sinkhole, pulling us toward oblivion. I thought I was just feeling dramatic, so I ignored it: turned on the radio, poured myself a glass of red wine, and set to making creamy cauliflower soup. But the strange shadow of something missing kept tugging, tapping me on the shoulder, saying, *Hey*, and refusing to go away until I succumbed. For the next two days, I baked batches upon batches of cherry coconut bars, fudge crumble bars, and marshmallow fudge cakes to give away to everyone I knew. I tried and tried to make date bars too, but they came out too hard or too syrupy, or the shortbread crumbled, and I just wanted her there with me to show me how to keep it all together.

—*For Karin, who came later*

11.
Dreams of Exclusive Breastfeeding

Mothering Without Enough Milk

GRACE M. CHO

In the beginning, before restaurants, before refrigerators, before kitchens, cookies or candy, there was our first hunger ... our first food and our first love.... As newborns, we take our first taste of mother's milk and forge our first bond with another human being.

—Marcus Samuelsson

I HAD NEVER BEEN ONE TO NATURALIZE motherhood, but when I was pregnant with my son, and only child, the sight of babies at their mothers' breasts began to make me well up with tears. Feeding others had always been one of my great joys in life, and doing so in such an intimate way began to occupy my daydreams. What I wanted more than anything was to do exclusive breast-feeding, or "EBF," as mothers on the Internet called it. My desire grew within a cultural moment that demanded this of mothers, but it also sprang from my background as a Korean immigrant and my training as a food studies scholar, concerned about the problems with industrialized food. No formula would ever touch my baby's lips, I thought. I would keep processed food away from him for as long as possible, which I had hoped to be about five years. I fantasized about the bonds that we would build together, one meal at a time.

As my pregnancy progressed, I daydreamed more and more about nursing my baby for the first time—that moment of bliss just seconds after giving birth to him. I imagined that seeing him emerge from my womb would be the most thrilling moment of my life and seeing him at my breast, seeking comfort and warmth, would be the most peaceful. What would I communicate to him in that moment, his first meal? That I would continue to be his world and provide whatever he needed and that I would feed him with my body. *Eat, eat. I made you dinner,* I would say with my touch. *We come from a long line of garlic eaters,* I would say with the slightly pungent sweetness of my milk. *And the other things you taste—the dark leafy greens, the oily fish, the super fruits, the herbs—those are things I've eaten for you. To make my milk as nutritionally potent as milk can be.* What I would communicate with that first meal was that I would give him the best possible start in life.

Just as I imagined nursing my baby for the first time, I imagined doing it for the thousandth time, perhaps somewhere in public, unashamed to bare my breasts. I imagined doing it for the five thousandth time when he no longer "needed" my milk, but I would continue to nurse well into his toddlerhood so that he could continue to have the armour against disease and the intimacy that comes from the warmth of his mother's breast. And what would I communicate then? That we were doing the same thing my mother and I once did, carrying on a family legacy of nursing your children until they can walk and talk. In my family, breastfeeding was an act of superior mothering and the ultimate expression of love. Like all the women in my family, I would do it for a long time.

> ...in informal conversation, several people said to me that women who breastfeed beyond a year are not doing it for the baby. They are doing extended breastfeeding because "they get something out of it." (Halley 100)

In the summer of 1972, my family moved from Busan, Korea, to my American father's hometown of five thousand people in rural Washington State. My mother had uprooted herself from her home to try to make a new one with my father in the fabled land of opportunity. There were many things that must have been stressful for her about this journey, but the one thing that stood out most to her was that on the eleven-hour transpacific flight, I demanded to nurse, and I did so relentlessly. At the age of one-and-a-half, I no longer needed her milk for nutrition, but my mother, like other Korean mothers of her time, had made no effort to wean me. My mother had barely left Korean airspace before she internalized a new set of cultural norms. Although she could not yet articulate what they were, she saw no other mothers nursing on the plane and knew that regardless of whether American mothers chose to feed from the breast or bottle, most of them would have raised an eyebrow at the sight of a toddler breastfeeding. Whereas in my mother's cultural frame of reference, it was normal and desirable to nurse a child until the age of three, four, or even five, in the U.S. it was considered pathological. On that flight, I screamed with rage when my mother denied me "*jomp-ti*," a pseudo-Korean word I had made up for my mother's breast. "Oh my god, you embarrassed me so much," she said as she told me the story years later. "The more I try to calm you down, the more you got mad. You just screaming for *jomp-ti, jomp-ti!* Then you grabbed my shirt and just ripped it open! My face got so red, wondering what people must think." These were the only details my mother ever shared with me about the day we moved to America.

I don't know how old I was when my mother weaned me, but I was old enough to remember it. I would go to her bedroom before dawn to tell her that I wanted *jomp-ti*, crawling into her lap and latching on to her nipple, the colour of nutmeg. She would rock me and stroke my hair and tell me that I was getting to be a big girl. "And big girls don't eat *jomp-ti*." We continued like this for some weeks or months, and one day I became vaguely aware that I was a big girl who was going to start school with other kids whose mothers didn't nurse them, a big girl who no longer needed *jomp-ti*.

According to the Committee on Nutritional Status During Pregnancy and Lactation, in 1972, the year my mother and I immigrated to the U.S., "the overall downward trend in breastfeeding incidence reached its nadir at 22 percent," and only 10 percent of American mothers nursed their infants longer than three months (30). The year 1973 marked the beginning of the trend's reversal from bottle back to breast, but mostly among white affluent women. In my town of working class whites, breastfeeding was never in fashion, and my mother, as the first brown-skinned immigrant woman in town, must have seemed even more backwards in the eyes of the other mothers who still believed that formula feeding was the proper method of feeding a baby. She was a minority in her child rearing practices as well as in her race and national origin.

Her transition to the U.S., an America that was not the one she had imagined, was more difficult than she had anticipated. She left Korea because she had been a woman who served American men in the bars around military bases. She had gone against gender and sexual norms, and this was socially unacceptable to the extent that her life in Korea had become unliveable. My mother was tired of being a misfit, and the United States represented the possibility of starting over. There were many ways in which my mother tried to conform to American customs and foodways, some of which she even internalized. Cheeseburgers, steak and potatoes, and pot roast became some of her favourite meals. We sat in chairs around a large elevated table rather than on the floor, cross-legged around a low little table. The Western table setting of plate, fork, and knife displaced the Korean one of bowls, spoons, and chopsticks. One food practice that my mother would not abandon, however, was that of nursing her babies until they were young children, old enough to start school.

My mother's capacity to feed others verged on the uncanny. She grew and foraged massive amounts of food. Even after sharing her bounty with friends and relatives, there was still such a large surplus, which she then sold and began to make a decent living from doing so. My mother always took great pride in her ability to produce food, but nothing made her more proud than the fact that she fed each of her children directly from her body for years. For my mother, breastfeeding was the foundation for good health, happiness and security. It was the basis for all her children's future successes.

Throughout the years, she made grand proclamations about the power of her milk, which I later understood as a form of self-validation for her unorthodox choices. When I brought home a stellar report card or won a spelling bee, she would say, "You know the reason why you so smart, don't you? Because I breastfed you so long." When, in the fourth grade, I was placed in a gifted and talented program, my mother said it again. "You know the reason why you so smart...." When, at the age of eleven, I had a growth spurt and shot up to five feet six inches, she attributed this, too, to the power of her milk. "You know the reason why you so tall, don't you?" My mother's milk was the source of all virtue. And as virtuous as my mother's milk was, she also communicated the idea that breastfeeding was part of our unique cultural and familial heritage, and that because of it we stood apart from the people among whom we lived. "I drank my mother's milk until I was five," she said once, blushing. "*Ah-merican* people must think it is weird." Above all, she loved to tell the story of our journey to the U.S. and the agonizing plane ride on which I drew attention to her breasts full of milk and her conspicuous otherness. "You screamed for *jomp-ti* and ripped my shirt open," she recounted again and again until it became part of the fibre of my consciousness.

> Perhaps you know women who claim that they didn't produce enough milk, that it wasn't rich enough, that their milk supply dried up one day.... The reason for this failure is rarely that the mother is unable to produce enough milk. (Huggins 4-5)

In the final weeks leading up to my due date, I prepared for my new role as a nursing mother by attending a breastfeeding class. The lactation consultant (LC) teaching the class, a bubbly white English woman in her mid-fifties, opened the session by asking a question: "Can anyone tell me why breast is best?" There was a silence in the room that no one wanted to break at first, so I raised my hand and said with absolute conviction, "Because human babies aren't designed to drink any other animal's milk." "Yes, very good. Babies are designed to drink mother's milk." A woman pregnant with twins raised concerns about not having enough milk for two babies, but the LC reassured her by talking about the miracles of lactation and the breast's capacity to make as much milk as the baby needs. The LC then asked participants to go around the room and each name a benefit of breastfeeding. I was the fifth person into the circle, and all the obvious benefits had already been named, so I took the opportunity to share the story about my mother's hyper-enthusiasm about breast milk. The rest of the class laughed, and I felt proud that my cultural background had put me so far ahead of the breastfeeding curve. More than anything, I realized how much my desire to breastfeed was tangled up in the loss of my mother. She had died a tragic death five years earlier, and breastfeeding my own child would help me to find her again.

When my baby's birthday finally came, it was far from the perfect moment I had imagined. He was born sixteen hours after my water broke, which revealed meconium in the fluid—"pea soup" as the doctors called it—after an excruciating night of listening to his heart rate decelerate with each contraction. He was then pulled from my womb by surgeons. I agreed to the Caesarean section because I believed that it probably was the safest way for him to come into the world, but I was overcome by grief and disappointment that I had been unable to give him a natural birth. I did not see him emerge from my body, nor did I get to hold him right after birth. The nurse put his cheek against mine before taking him away, and I waited for what seemed like a long time, as the doctors finished sewing up the three layers of flesh that they had cut open before I got to nurse my baby. I vaguely remember someone (a nurse?) laying him on my chest as my doula guided me. I awkwardly pushed aside the wires that were attached to my body to help him find his way to my nipple, and I was so high on drugs that I was hardly aware of what it felt like.

A few weeks later, as I nursed my new baby, I had a revelation. My right arm cradled his tiny body, and I nudged him ever closer to my chest as if to bring him back inside, to let him know that there was still time for us to be one. It was a chilly night in late November, and we lay together in bed without blankets or pillows so that there would be no risk of his getting caught in them. The only warmth came from our bodies. I watched his little mouth fluttering in beats of three. Suck, suck, suck, pause. Suck, suck, suck, pause—the rhythm of comfort before falling asleep. As we lay there together floating off to dream, I suddenly became overwhelmed by a flood of emotion. *Savour this moment*, I whispered to myself. *Savour this moment because it will be gone in the blink of an eye. Savour this moment*, I repeated as if the repetition of the words could make it happen. *But I can't*, I responded to myself.

By the time I realize it's happening the moment is already gone. All our awareness is only of the past. I sobbed for a while before finishing the conversation with myself. *Then remember. Remember this moment of nursing your baby. Remember this tiny creature at your breast. Remember this feeling. Remember ... for as long as you live. Remember....*

There were other nights when I lay in bed with my baby and cried. It was usually while I was talking to him, making promises that I couldn't keep. *I'll always protect you, my love. Mommy will never leave you,* I'd say, knowing full well that these were lies. One day I would die, and our whole lives together would be a process of gradually and finally letting go. I cried many times, overwhelmed by the fragility of life and the limits of being human, but there was something different about the night I tried to sear the memory of him nursing into my mind. That night, my whole being ached with longing as if I knew that we were nearing the end.

A few days later, my dreams of exclusive breastfeeding turned into a nightmare. Instead of nursing, my baby fussed. Then the fussing turned into wailing. He seemed hungry, but no matter what I did, I could not get him to nurse. The next day, I went to a breastfeeding support group at the hospital where I had given birth. The LC running the group was a brusque-mannered white woman with a raspy smoker's voice. I remembered her from the hospital after I had given birth when the LCs had made their rounds to visit the new mothers. The first two were warm and encouraging. But not this one. All of her observations sounded like accusations. "He's not latched on! He's just on the nipple!" she said in an exasperated tone. "Try again." I was less than thrilled to see her at the group.

There were three other mothers there with their babies, ranging from two to ten weeks. The mother of the two-week-old said that her daughter didn't want to nurse at all and then pulled a bottle of formula out of her bag. "It's because of the bottle," barked the LC. "Instant gratification. Why work for something if you can get it for free?" The baby started to fuss as the woman offered her breast. "Calm her down first. Hold her to your chest and let her listen to your heartbeat. Now give her the bottle." The baby drank ravenously and the LC intervened. "Just enough to calm her down!" I watched the scene unfold with bewilderment: the

LC would support formula feeding, despite her disapproval of the bottle's "instant gratification." I had been under the impression that the need for formula was extremely rare.

Another mother spoke about challenges of feeding her baby from a supplementer—a special feeding tube that is taped to the mother's nipple and attached to a bottle containing milk or formula. "It's like a straw," she said as she puckered her lips and made a sucking motion. The whole notion of supplementing was new to me, and I was surprised to encounter these other mothers who were feeding their newborn babies formula. When it was my turn, I explained that my baby had been fussy while nursing, and I asked if the LC could take a look at his latch. "We don't check for latch here. This is just a support group," she said. Then I weighed him. At his last doctor's appointment, my baby's weight gain had been right on track, but since then he had hardly gained any weight. The LC frowned at me. "You have to take him to the doctor right away. If you can't get an appointment, take him to the emergency room. He could be malnourished." Emergency room? Malnourished? I became paralyzed with fear and shame at the thought that my child could be malnourished.

I promptly consulted another LC who determined that my baby was only getting about half the milk that he needed. She gave me a few ideas for increasing my supply, and both she and the doctor recommended supplementing the milk with formula in the meantime. Barely four weeks old, my baby was going to start on a formula diet, the very thing I was certain would never happen. The next day was Thanksgiving, but instead of feasting, I sat on the couch and cried, grieving the loss of my ability to nourish my baby and to do what I believed was so important. I had long ago internalized my mother's voice, championing the virtues of breastfeeding, and there I sat, feeling as if I had disappointed her. I imagined her making a fuss over the formula and wondering what was wrong that I had so little milk.

I began my regimen of nursing then pumping, nursing then pumping, eight to ten times a day. Increasing my milk supply became my new obsession. I frequented several websites and online communities dedicated to increasing milk supply, and in doing so, learned that I was not alone in either my difficulties or my feelings. Well-intentioned friends had told me not to worry because "formula-fed babies turn out fine." One even pointed out that the politics of breastfeeding was designed to "make women feel like shit if they can't do it." Although I agreed, putting my personal struggles within a political framework felt like a denial of my grief. I preferred to be in conversation with other mothers who understood the complex feelings of loss that accompany breastfeeding failure. One woman said that it had been her "lifelong dream to EBF." The phrase resonated with me because of my own experience of having been told my whole life that breast is best.

Nearly all the resources that I had consulted said that low milk supply was rare, so I hoped that mine would be short lived. I tried a whole slew of galactogogues— fenugreek, blessed thistle, alfalfa, raspberry leaf, nettles, seaweed, oatmeal, flax, Brewer's yeast, goat's rue, shatavari. I also sought treatment from an acupuncturist and Chinese herbalist. My supply did increase, but only proportionally to my son's needs. Seven weeks later I sought the advice of another LC. This one diagnosed my baby with tongue-tie, which explained why he had been unable to nurse efficiently. The doctor who clipped his tongue told me that she was unsure about increasing my milk supply at that point, but maybe I wouldn't have to pump anymore. I did continue to pump, however. Two weeks later, with a new combination of herbs and extra pumping sessions between feedings, my milk supply had hardly changed. Then I pulled out the last stop—domperidone, an anti-emetic drug whose side effect was increased milk production. It was not approved by the U.S. Food and Drug Administration and therefore expensive and hard to get. I took it for six weeks and it increased my supply a little but not enough to stop the formula. I simply couldn't make enough milk.

Tell me what you eat and I'll tell you who you are.
(Brillat-Savarin)

By the time my son was six months old, I became resigned to the fact that my dreams of EBF would never be fulfilled. I still had regrets, but at the same time consoled myself by knowing that I tried everything, that he was healthy, and that I had been able to give him some breast milk every day of his life. I still wondered what would have happened if someone had caught his tongue-tie when he was first born. What if I had starting pumping as soon as I got home from the hospital? What if I hadn't trusted the conventional wisdom that your body could make enough milk?

Six months also began another phase of eating—the introduction of solids. It was a second chance to show him that homemade meals are better than food made by corporations and a second chance to continue my family tradition. *Miyeok-guk* was one of his favourites, and one of mine, too. I fed him *bibimbap* with mushrooms and told him of foraging adventures with my mother. I gave him little tastes of salty fish with rice, one of the first meals that I can remember eating. I still sometimes grieved over the missed opportunities in our breastfeeding relationship, but I also reminded myself that I was still able to feed him from my body because now I was feeding him my memories.

WORKS CITED

Brillat-Savarin, Jean Anthelme. *The Physiology of Taste: Or Meditations on Transcendental Gastronomy*. Transl. Fayette Robinson. Digireads.com, 2004. E-book.

Committee on Nutritional Status During Pregnancy and Lactation, Institute of Medicine. *Nutrition During Lactation*. Washington DC: The National Academies Press, 1991. Print.

Halley, Jean O'Malley. *The Boundaries of Touch: Parenting and Adult-Child Intimacy*. Champaign: University of Illinois Press, 2009. Print.

Huggins, Kathleen R.N., M.S. *The Nursing Mother's Companion*. Cambridge: The Harvard Common Press, 1999. Print.

The Meaning of Food. Dir. Kris Kristenson. Perf. Marcus Samuelsson. PBS, 2005. DVD.

III.
Negotiating Intercultural Maternal Experiences

12.
Lebkuchen Lesson

Teaching Our Children Through Traditional Foods

EMILY WEISKOPF-BALL

THROUGH A REFLECTION ON THE ISSUE of traditional food, this chapter is firstly a manifesto, a call to action, a plea to all parents to dig through the dusty recesses of their brains to recollect the traditional food of their youth.[1] Armed with these nourishing thoughts, I urge you to ignore, at crucial times of the year and in small doses, the dominant discourse of our age that makes "healthy" food one of the markers of good parenting. I don't mean to suggest that you should overindulge in sugar or forget about fruits, vegetables, and whole grains altogether. However, this chapter argues that making and sharing special treats with children not only is an important aspect of motherhood, but that maintaining these customs also allows mothers to teach their children about their heritage and to create memories that their children will carry with them into the future. By consuming family favourites at specific times of the year, we all, essentially, reaffirm specific versions of ourselves. If these foods disappear, we lose a part of our past and make it difficult to maintain these aspects of who we are.

My realization that it is important to break some of society's ideas of proper mothering came to me on the morning of December 6, 2013. For German-speaking children around the world, December 6 is Saint Nicholas's Day. The night before, children polish a pair of their best shoes and place one of them outside their bedroom door. During the night, Saint Nicholas comes and leaves all deserving children a *Lebkuchen*, a German cookie shaped as him as well as some chocolate [figure 1]. At least, this is how my family has always celebrated it. On December 6, 2013, my daughters, then

Figure 1

three and one, were ecstatic. My eldest found her shoe first and then quickly woke her sister up to show her hers. Both then rushed to their father to show him. Picture the genuine elation on their faces. Hear the sound of excited footsteps pounding up and down the hallway. Imagine the barely comprehensible, high-pitched, monosyllabic words of a one-year-old trying to explain the magical appearance of a cookie in her shoe. The moment was one of pure joy—a joy equivalent to Christmas morning. In the darkness of the winter morning, their happiness lit up the room and brought a smile to my face.

As they settled down, they asked if they could eat their cookies. Instinctively, I said "No." Then I watched as their smiles turned into frowns of confusion. Their shoulders fell. They asked "Why?" And I didn't have a good answer. At least, not one that they would have understood. How could I tell them that they could not eat their cookies because I was afraid it would be viewed unfavourably by others? Sugar reputably makes kids hyper and although I had never noticed this adverse effect in my children, I had noticed it others. Of course, I didn't want my kids to give the daycare workers a hard time. I didn't want to be labelled a bad mother for having filled my children with treats. I wanted to conform. But in those seconds, as I tried to come up with a rational answer to give my girls, I realized that if they didn't eat their cookies for breakfast, they might never eat them at all. If the cookies caused them to be too hyper for daycare, then we couldn't have them for desserts either as the sugar might make them too hyper for bed. If I had sent the cookies to daycare, I would have caused conflict between the kids and the employees because daycare didn't allow outside food. I could have waited for the weekend, but by then the magic of the moment would have absolutely faded away.

In those seconds, I was transported to my own childhood and remembered eating the cookies for breakfast. I remembered how this European tradition made me feel special because my Canadian friends were not permitted such indulgences. I thought of my mother, who had made the cookies, and of her certain disappointment if she had learned that they had gone to waste. I thought of my Oma, who had been keeping this tradition alive since she had immigrated to Canada in 1960. I thought of the tradition itself, of this defining feature of my cultural heritage, and realized that if I said no to eating the cookie, I was also saying no to a part of who I am and, moreover, that I was denying my daughters that piece of themselves. In that moment, I rebelled against society and its discourse. I said "Yes" and then allowed them to eat as much of the cookie that they wanted and to eat the chocolate snowmen that Saint Nicholas had also left.

Some might find that I am being slightly overdramatic. It's only a cookie, you might say. If it disappears, it's no big deal. But this is no ordinary cookie. *Lebkuchen* cannot be purchased in North Bay, Ontario. It must be made from scratch. A strong commitment must exist to keep this tradition alive in Northern Ontario. This cookie represents a love for not only your children but also for your cultural heritage and personal identity.

Although it tastes somewhat similar to gingerbread, *Lebkuchen* has a distinct flavour. To make it, heat 450 grams of Lyle's Golden Syrup, 50 grams of butter, and 100 grams of sugar. Once the sugar dissolves, it can be transferred to a bowl and a ½ teaspoon of cinnamon, ½ teaspoon of ground cloves, ¼ teaspoon of allspice, and 1 teaspoon of almond extract must be added. Once the mixture has cooled enough, add 1 egg, 4 teaspoons of baking powder, and 500 grams of flour.[2] Although some of this mixing can be done with a machine, the dough is sticky and eventually needs to be mixed with a spoon. Rolling it is also tricky. Put enough flour on the counter and the rolling pin so that the dough doesn't cling to it. Yet, playing with the dough too much will cause the dough to become hard.

Figure 2

The figure must be traced first on a cardboard template and then cut into the dough. The cookie must be moved cautiously to keep the shape from shifting. In my family, the size of the cookie depends on the age of the child. For the first few years, the cookie is roughly the size of a large gingerbread man. By the time one is an adult, however, the cookie is roughly twelve inches tall [figure 2]. This means that various-sized templates must be made. Decorating the cookie is also complicated. The figure must first be painted with a light brown icing and then outlined with a pinkish hue icing. This colour can be achieved with food colouring, but a healthier and more traditional method is to add the juice of crushed raspberries. Saint Nicholas holds a sprig of *lycopodium*, a green plant, which must be gathered in the woods, and the details of his tunic must be made of white icing The Oma, or grandmother, is responsible for making the cookies for all of her grandchildren until they turn eighteen. At that point, the mother takes over making the cookies for her own children. My Oma, for a period of time, made seventeen cookies a year: for her and her husband, her three children, their spouses, and her nine grandchildren. My own mother now makes fourteen a year. Thus the cookie maker must tailor her recipe from year to year to meet her family's needs. These have to be made when young children aren't around. To mask the cookies' distinct smell, both my Oma and my mother make a special Christmas cake with many of the same spices so children do not grow suspicious [figure 3]. Despite these seemingly strict rules, my family's *Lebkuchen* cannot be mass produced. Using a template rather than a cutter means that each cookie will be unique. Furthermore, there is also room to be creative with the design. The figure's hat, for example, can be purposely tiled, the way my mother does, to give him a

Figure 3

whimsical look. The piping can be done in different sizes and embellished if desired. If *lycopodium* is hard to find, a regional plant may be substituted for it. Thus not only do the cookies tell important stories about the people receiving them, but they also reveal telling clues about their makers.

In this fast-paced society, it might seem ridiculous to put so much effort into a traditional food that is so tedious and time consuming to make. The dough is difficult to work with, Lyle's Golden Syrup is often hard to find in grocery stores, and the chocolate figures and coins Saint Nicholas leaves behind can make this tradition expensive. Eliminating this ritual could be seen as no big deal. Indeed, some might argue that this cookie making is just another example of the unpaid labour that mothers are expected to do. Indeed, motherhood has always been a complex and multifaceted job that has long involved food making as one of its central tenants. In her article "Writing Women: The Virtual Cookbook and Pinterest," Amy Brooke Antonio states that food making has been associated with women "[a]s a result of the Fall ... [when] Adam was instructed to work, and Eve was punished with the pain of childbearing and motherhood." Since Western society has historically drawn many of its founding principles from the Bible, and specifically the Book of Genesis, "[t]raditionalist assumptions [have] posited that the assignment of different tasks and roles to men and women was evidence of the naturalness of their respective responsibilities." The view that cooking is women's "natural" duty has in fact long been central to the gendered division of household labour (McKenna 10). Even if more and more men are taking on these roles, as the many personal stories in *Man with a Pan: Culinary Adventures of Fathers Who Cook for their Families* clearly testify, given the historical precedent, it is not surprising that contemporary mothers are still largely the ones held accountable for their children's food habits.

Lost in all of the discussion about sugar and obesity is that children must also be fed metaphorically wholesome food that comes in the shape of memories. In her article "Food for the Soul," cardiologist Cynthia Thaik argues that the best food of all consists of "gratitude, appreciation, self-love and love of others, laughter, joy, [and] mindfulness" while bad food includes "self-doubt, judgement, fear, anticipation, anger, [and] hatred." Traditional foods, like *Lebkuchen*, can be either a positive or a negative food-stuff. If mothers react negatively to the food of their childhood, as I almost did with my daughters, the cookie becomes a symbol of self-doubt and judgment. With time and repeated exposure, children internalize these messages and also make negative associations between the food and the culture. Similarly, if mothers fill themselves with negative thoughts of guilt and self-doubt, they will eventually give up practices that should bring everyone joy and happiness. Traditional food is not everyday food and it is precisely because of its distinction from the common that it should be included in our yearly and/or seasonal menus. Framed in this positive way, traditional food should be valued rather than rejected. Thaik shares that "[l]aughter relaxes muscles and releases tension. It causes physiological changes that have been compared to a mild workout. It increases blood flow and improves sleep, making it easier for your physical body to restore itself." For her, "[j]oy means finding something worth celebrating ... [such as] prepar[ing] a particularly satisfying and delicious meal." In other words, we must also eat, as my Oma insists, food that is good for the soul. In moderation, and at special times of the year, we need to eat food that makes us happy. Moments, like Saint Nicholas morning, the culmination of hours spent preparing the surprise cookies, are physically, mentally, and emotionally satisfying as they nourish the soul with gratitude, appreciation, self-love and the love of others, laughter, joy, and mindfulness.

The loss of a treasured recipe underscores the void that is created when the ability to recreate a favourite taste is lost. I have witnessed this on numerous occasions. The first time was when I was still a teenager. Our dog ate our recipe for giant oatmeal chocolate chip cookies. Despite hours spent online and in cookbooks to find a replacement, we have not found a cookie that has come close to the perfect texture and taste of that specific recipe. I witnessed another example of such a loss when my mother tried, unsuccessfully, to find a recipe for her grandmother's molasses cookies. In her mind, being a grandmother meant making those cookies, and she wanted to share her definition and memory of grandmotherhood with the next generation. The numerous stories in *Storied Dishes: What Our Family Recipes Tell Us About Who We Are and Where We've Been* as well as recent autobiographical and ethnographic works such as Diane Tye's *Baking as Biography* attest to the power that food has in creating a network between women and between generations. When we are interested in our past but are missing information about where we come from and why we are the way we are, we can turn to our mothers' recipes for clues (Tye). Indeed, as Renee Marton suggests in "Cakewalk," making a family favourite is a "way of embodying a family ideal ... [the] actions fulfill personal, cultural, and even physical expectation" (23). In today's quinoa-bread consuming, lentil-loving world where chocolate cake is sometimes made with zucchini and contains little to no chocolate at all, we must not forget the age old adage that we are, to a certain extent, what we eat. These physical reenactments sustain us by connecting us to others and, moreover, ground us in our space and in our selves.

Making traditional food does not mean giving up healthy food or becoming a radical resistor of socially accepted ideas of being healthy and/or of motherhood. Indeed, by resisting certain aspects of the dominant discourse on motherhood but sill accepting others, the participants of Erika Horwitz's and Reva Seth's studies ultimately illustrate that what constitutes "good" rests perhaps more with the individual mother than on a collectively accepted version of motherhood. The decisions a mother makes, after all, depend on a number of factors, including the following: her age, socio-economic class, marital status, living environment, the number of children in the family, and the pressure that comes from other mothers, other members of the family, and the media.

Through this reflective chapter on traditional food habits, I hope to have convinced all readers of the importance of keeping the past alive by passing on to their children the foods and memories of their youth. Good parenting, being a good mother, comes from creating positive, life-affirming, value-laden memories with one's children. Guilt, a common element of motherhood, certainly extends to food choices. However, the importance of keeping heritage alive should override feelings of guilt about serving certain treats. Recipes are not only words on paper to be read. They are meant to be shared physically and sensually. If they stop circulating, not only in written form but also through our bodies, their power and pedagogy die.

We also need to be aware of the power these moments have on our children by observing how they embody the principles that the foods stand for. While I was making waffles for dinner, another tradition that comes from the German side of my family, my youngest daughter insisted that her Morgan-doll come sit on the counter with her to witness what was happening. As I finished cooking the batter, I watched her carefully hold Morgan's flimsy fabric body beside her. Morgan then also sat with us as we ate. After dinner, she pulled Morgan off the table to show her the ducks on the lawn. If a mother's job is to feed her children nourishing food that provides sustenance for their bodies and their souls, then I'm happy that my daughters are consuming the sweet values that I have carried on from my childhood: sharing, joy, inclusion, and empathy.

All images courtesy of the author.

ENDNOTES

[1] I would like to take this opportunity to thank Dr. Linda M. Ambrose, Dr. Joël Belliveau, and Dr. Ernst Gerhardt of Laurentian University for their many hours of support and for their helpful suggestions regarding my work. I would also like to thank my family for their reflections and stories.

[2] I would like to thank my Oma, Helga Weiskopf, for allowing me to contribute this treasured and closely guarded family recipe. I

would also like to thank my Maman, Carmen Weiskopf, for allowing me to include her cookie template, instructions, and pictures.

WORKS CITED

Brooke Antonio, Amy "Writing Women: The Virtual Cookbook and Pinterest." *M/C Journal* 16.3 (2013). Web. 10 August 2014.

DeVault, Marjorie. *Feeding the Family: The Social Organization of Caring as Gendered Work*. Chicago: University of Chicago Press, 1991. Print

Donohue, John. Ed. *Man with a Pan: Culinary Adventures of Fathers Who Cook for Their Families*. Chapel Hill: Algonquin Books of Chapel Hill, 2011. Print.

Horwitz, Erika. *Through the Maze of Motherhood: Empowered Mothers Speak*. Bradford, Ontario: Demeter Press, 2011. Print.

Marton, Renee. "Cakewalk." *Storied Dishes: What Our Family Recipes Tell Us About Who We Are and Where We've Been*. Ed. Linda Murray Berzok. Santa Barbara: Praeger, 2011. 23-25. Print.

McKenna, Katherine. *A Life of Propriety: Anne Murray Powell and Her Family, 1755-1849*. Montreal: McGill-Queen's Press, 1994. Print.

Seth, Reva. *The MomShift: Women Share their Stories of Career Success After Having Children*. Canada: Random House Canada, 2014. Print.

Thaik, Cynthia, Dr. "Foods for the Soul." *Psychology Today: Health, Help, Happiness + Find a Therapist*. 1 Apr. 2013. Web. 18 Aug. 2014.

Tye, Diane. *Baking As Biography*. Canada: Mc-Gill-Queen University Press, 2010. Print.

13.
Scary Candy, Goldfish Crackers, and Kale Chips

Feeding and Parenting
Our New Canadian Daughter in Toronto

FLORENCE PASCHE GUIGNARD AND THOMAS GUIGNARD

IN THIS PIECE, WE EXPLORE, from a dual perspective, selected aspects of our family's adaptation to new cultural norms of parenting and of feeding our child in the multicultural urban environment of Toronto to which we moved about three years ago. As the lead narrator, Florence reflects on occasions when she becomes aware, as a mother and as a newcomer to Canada, of how choices regarding food and mealtimes affect her mothering and vice versa. Her narrative is enriched by the interventions of her husband, Thomas (evidenced in italics), that bring in consistent or diverging views or experience with similar topics.

SCARY CANDY
HALLOWEEN 2014

Trick or treat, smell my feet
Gimme something good to eat...

Scary characters come to knock at our door: a few vampires, a bunch of ghosts, witches, princesses, superheroes, and many others. This is our third Halloween in Canada, the country where we relocated for me to complete my postdoctoral research. It is also the country where Thomas was born; however, since he moved back to Switzerland with his parents at the age of four, his experience of arriving in Canada is very similar to mine. This year, we have decided to not play by the rules of the game: we will not hand out high-fructose corn syrup, GMO, and dye-laden candy to the children coming to trick or treat at the apartment that we rent. Last year, I felt self-conscious about this. I am still not sure that distributing scary stickers, tattoos, and cheap plastic toys from the dollar store, which we will hand out this year, is a politically correct alternative or even a more environmentally and socially sustainable one. I acknowledge that this is an imperfect compromise. Whichever choices we make as consumers, as parents, as participants in society, some level of contradiction will persist.

I feel sad that I cannot bake treats for the children myself. Another mother explained to me that most trick-or-treaters will only accept packaged candy as anything homemade might look suspicious and get thrown away. Tonight, I will let our daughter Fiona collect from other households certain foodstuffs that I would not readily buy myself, and I am expected to give other children products that I wish neither to purchase nor to consume. Beyond the consumption and health issues, I am mostly concerned about already breaking up with a cultural tradition that I am embracing ambivalently in the first place.

Our daughter is dressed as Queen Elsa, the widely successful Disney character of the year. I made her costume from bits and pieces from the thrift store and "do-it-yourselfer" Thomas provided her with a laser-cut snowflake sceptre of his own design. To hosts complimenting her on her outfit, Fiona is quick to reply "No, I am *not* a princess.... I am a queen!" The concept of a queen begging door to door is paradoxical, as is Halloween to me. Dressing up is the fun part of this tradition, which I enjoy. It reminds me of Carnival. But why add the candy? Not just *a little bit* of symbolic candy, but (plastic orange) buckets full of it, as far as I can see. After she comes back from her night spree, the queen will deposit part of her candy in a plate, but by the morning, the Switch Witch will have exchanged it for a non-edible gift. If the Tooth Fairy exists, and if Coca-Cola can reinvent Santa Claus, why can't a mother make up a new tradition for the sake of fun, healthy teeth, and nutrition? Later, I will learn that I am not the only one who came up with such an idea and that other parents, too, are seeking alternatives. In the U.S., some dentists even buy the candy back from children, rewarding them with money and a toothbrush. The dentists then send the potentially harmful lollipops to the military serving abroad.

As a newcomer, I perceive other paradoxes around food and parenting in the Halloween tradition. For the other 364 days of the year, our child may not indiscriminately accept any type of food from strangers for several reasons. Recently, we found out that she is allergic to sesame.

Unfortunately, Fiona's food allergy must be part of the genetic legacy she inherited from me, as I have learned to live with this condition since my teenage years and now have to carry an EpiPen with me at all times. Although my own first allergic reaction was more traumatic, the first hint of her sensitivity came as we were preparing dinner together. As I often do, I encouraged her to try the various ingredients we were handling that night, including the tahini sesame paste that I was adding to hummus. She complained of feeling an itch in her mouth, something that occurred again a few days later when eating a sesame snack bar. Fortunately, her reaction to sesame so far has been mild and has not led to anaphylactic shock. She was quick to understand that she had to avoid eating food with sesame because she knew that her dad also had a list of foods he should avoid. Explaining that sesame was making her throat itch and could potentially be dangerous, we taught her to ask for the ingredients when she is offered food. We thought it important that she be aware of her condition and the potential consequences, and learn how to be careful with what she eats rather than relying entirely on caregivers, other parents, and us enquiring on her behalf about food offered to her outside of home. We know we cannot protect her from everything. Through food, nutrition, and many other things, we are teaching her responsibility.

Is feeding the children of other parents a privilege or an obligation? Tonight, for Halloween, I am sending our daughter to more or less known and friendly neighbours to solicit candy that I will not let her eat entirely. In the midst of the dark night, of what was originally the Celtic celebration of Samhain, the Switch Witch will take away most of her Halloween candy loot. Another part will be recycled into an Advent calendar, a European Christian tradition that I am eager to introduce her to. For the twenty-four days preceding Christmas, she will receive one surprise per day, not just candy or chocolate but also small inedible items, such as new pencils, buttons, or hairbands.

The preconceptions about what constitutes "good parenting" that I have internalized, growing up in Switzerland in a particular socio-economic context, clash with what I perceive as new expectations. The choice to adhere to them is mine to some extent. My integration among other parents in this neighbourhood somehow depends on it. I would not feel like a "good mother" if my daughter gets cavities or becomes sick because of what she eats. Damages to a child's health—whether cavities or morbid obesity—is often considered a maternal failure, rarely a paternal one. However, I would feel bad not letting her participate in Halloween and in other traditions new to me that involve edible items (like receiving "loot bags" with candy after birthday parties). When I relinquish to others the power to feed my child, I still keep the responsibility of the outcomes. Over time, I have learned to relax about this: trick-or-treating is not an everynight activity and sugary Easter eggs or chocolate bunnies are not a daily staple in our household either. A little, occasional, sugar won't harm my child's long-term health, but I would prefer that this sugar would come from home-cooked treats.

Although I share my wife's concerns about providing our child with a healthy diet and lifestyle, I realize I am far less sensitive than she is when it comes to comparing our parenting with what might be expected by caregivers, other parents, and family. I admit to being much less affected by the implicit social pressure she reports feeling when discussing our daughter with others. I view my role as a parent to be one of teaching my child the values in which I believe, along with a critical mind that will hopefully allow her later to question those values and choose her own. This process is, in my opinion, far more important than conforming to the "good parenting" practices or "good nutrition" advice of the time, most of which will probably have become obsolete by the next generation.

Even though I was born in Canada, I was not raised here and so share Florence's experience of being a newcomer. Because we spent our childhood in another country, there are many aspects of what it means to be a child growing up in Canada that we only learned through literature and other media: we never experienced them firsthand. PA and pyjama days, school fundraisers, book drives and show-and-tell sessions were never fully explained to the novice parents that we are, often leaving us wondering what was expected of us or our child. The abundance of extracurricular activities, however, sometimes felt more like a test of our parenting skills than a novelty. The existence of little league soccer was revealed to us only when our daughter asked why all her friends got to wear a Tim Horton's shirt and gathered to play every week, and not her. By that time, even if we could have fitted the weekly practice in our family schedule, registration had long closed. The next winter, when I tried to register her for skating classes, I was dismayed to find out that all spots had been taken by 8:00 am on the day that registration opened. Only when I mentioned this to other parents did I learn how sought after those programs were and what the best strategy was to secure them.

"And what is your daughter doing? Ballet, swimming, martial arts? What about grammar classes?" Such innocuous questions cast doubts on our parenting skills. In the small mountain villages in Switzerland where we grew up, outdoor activities were for the most part unorganized—no need to register at 7:00 am two months in advance to play ball in the neighbour's field. We spend time cooking, playing, and walking with her, teaching her how to ride her bike, visiting museums, and taking her to the Maker Faire. Compared with the complex weekly schedule of Fiona's friends, however, these activities seem paltry, and we wonder if we will ever be up to the standards of good parenting in North America.

CULINARY COSMOPOLITANS

Some immigrants to Canada immediately identify and solve the challenges that they face, such as maintaining a purely vegetarian, kosher, or halal diet as well as finding rare ingredients for specific home recipes. As newcomers from Europe, we had not expected that we would have to rethink this intersection of parenting and foodways to such an extent. We needed some time to find our marks in the rich and multicultural foodscape of Toronto, which we have come to enjoy immensely. Growing up in rural areas of

Switzerland in the 1980s and 1990s, we had little experience, as children, of tasting food then dubbed "exotic." Our mothers rarely prepared "international" dishes.

A small, landlocked territory, Switzerland has nevertheless sat at the intersection of major trading routes for centuries. Its diet has constantly evolved to include exotic ingredients such as the saffron that is found in several traditional types of bread. Italian, French, and German influences are quite apparent in dishes that have a long documented presence in the country, a trend that was reinforced by subsequent waves of immigration. Until recently, however, the majority of migrants to Switzerland were of European origin. As a result, Asian or Latin American cuisines are a relatively recent addition. I remember first tasting sushi in my late teens and experiencing the disastrous result of eating a whole dab of grated wasabi without knowing what it was. My first encounter with soy sauce was during a visit to Canada at age fifteen.

I do not remember eating sushi or tacos, for instance, until my early twenties. I am glad that our daughter gets the chance to be exposed to new tastes and new ways of eating. I also know that this cultural diversity is selective and curated. Fiona already knows how to eat properly with a fork, but she also tries to use chopsticks and eats Ethiopian *injera* with her fingers. For her, it will be "normal" to have access to burritos, *pierogi, bibimbap* and other foods, which we have grown fond of, but were not part of our diet just over three years ago. This is probably not the case, however, for all children in Toronto or in Canada in general. We are privileged to have access to almost any type of food while, in the same city, some parents worry not about *what* they will eat, but *how* they will pay for their next meal.

Our daughter has been exposed to all sorts of "exotic" foods from a very young age and even more so since we moved to Canada. We encourage Fiona to try out everything, telling her that it is perfectly okay not to like a certain type of food but that she needs to try it first. Through foods from different origins, she becomes aware of cultural diversity and accepts it as a normal element of life. I am convinced that moving to Toronto has made this important step in her development easier, as the city is currently still more culturally diverse than Switzerland.

I am curious to know what happens, in a big urban centre like Toronto, to children exposed to such culinary diversity, and how their parents play a role in introducing them to a vast array of foods or in discouraging them from tasting unfamiliar dishes. Going beyond the necessary "food literacy" that many are now advocating for, could teaching children through and about food diversity be a way to promote both the maintenance of distinct culinary heritages and intercultural awareness? Rather than enforcing a form of "culinary citizenship" (Mannur 29) or "culinary nationalism" (Parkhurst Ferguson 29) on our child, I seek to introduce her to diversity. As journalist Adam McDowell notes, "... in the real world, the diversity of culinary heritage isn't disappearing, it's arriving on our plates all at once." Globalization does not imply that we have to give up the pride and skills associated with cuisines linked to specific territories or ingredients. I make sure that our daughter will grow to also appreciate typically Swiss dishes, such as *raclette* and *fondue*. Here, "our" food is the "exotic," or, at least, unusual food. I also try to convey to her that mealtime is about nutrition, indeed, but it is foremost about taste and pleasure, and about being social. I do not believe that it is necessary for all members of a large community to all eat the same thing at the same time in the same way to achieve the commendable goal of *"vivre ensemble,"* living together. However, as a smaller social unit, and foremost as a family, I insist that we spend time eating together, preferably the same dish, leaving some space for accommodation as long as it does not burden the cook.

During our first six weeks in Toronto, we rented a furnished downtown loft studio that unexpectedly taught us something important. The apartment had a kitchen and a prep area, but no dining table. After being forced to eat all our meals awkwardly on a couch and coffee table for over a month, we came to realize how central taking meals together was for our life as a family. Reproducing values we were taught by our parents, we believe that the "table comes first" (Gopnik), not only at the restaurant but also in the family home. With the exception of workday lunches, we try to eat all our meals together at the dinner table, sitting down. Eating breakfasts alone on the kitchen counter at the time most convenient for each family member, a practice that seems more

*common in North America, feels out of place, even if we admit it
could potentially smooth out busy weekday mornings.*

GOLDFISH CRACKERS

Why did I become so upset about goldfish crackers? It is about 5:45
pm and I have just picked up our daughter from the daycare where
she started going to a few weeks ago. The caregivers are doing
a pretty good job and our then three-year-old feels comfortable
meeting other kids and learning English. Within just a few months
after our arrival, she sings songs, knows the alphabet, and plays
with other children in a brand new language. Two years later, while
playing with her little toy kitchen, she takes orders from her dolls
and stuffies in English. Rapidly, too, she learns about new eating
habits, some of which contradict what we strive to practise at home.

This late afternoon, I can see that my child is really tired. I am
trying to figure out why she is whining so much. Before I can even
intervene, one of her caregivers asks her if she wants a snack. A
snack? I cringe. Now? Didn't she have one at 4:00 pm already?
Too late! Already, she has in her hand a small package of goldfish
crackers. "It's okay, they are peanut-free!" says the caregiver. I
could not care less that they are peanut-free. This is not the issue.
The point is that I am upset that someone distributes food to my
child in front of me without my permission and right before dinner.
I am worried that this will spoil her appetite and that she then will
not eat what I have prepared, not just for her but for the whole
family. I do not know how to react. Taking the now-opened bag
of crackers out of her hand certainly will not help resolve the situation, nor will it improve my child's mood. And I am afraid that
the caregiver might take offense if we refuse her "gift." It is not
that a few goldfish crackers are bad, but they are so untimely in my
opinion. I disagree with food being regularly used as an emotional
comfort. I suggest that Fiona pick three little fish out of the bag,
hand it back to her generous caregiver, and thank her for sharing.

*Offering snacks to children throughout the day feels to us con-
trary to the importance we give to family meal times. While we
recognize that children can require more than three meals a day, we
try to have organized snack times (again, reproducing the morning*

147

"dix heures" (10:00 am) and afternoon "quatre heures" (4:00 pm) snack breaks we had growing up). We are still uncomfortable with the concept of the "snack drawer" that seems common in the households of many of Fiona's friends, and we discourage her from snacking at odd hours, especially close to meal times.

The three little goldfish crackers worked their effect: food distracted my daughter and now we can walk home and make dinner. Should I fuss over the goldfish crackers or yield and accept that food can be effectively used as emotional bribery? The "maternal thinking" (Ruddick) that I engage in constantly weighs the short-term consequences with the long-term ones that result from creating a habit. I am confronting my maternal perspective on how I wish to feed my child, balancing the pleasure in having timely, tasty, and aesthetically looking foods with what is socially acceptable in Canada in terms of feeding and mothering children. I still cannot help also considering what is required from a child and her mother in our country of origin. If Swiss relatives label my child a picky eater, this will be considered a failure in the food education that I am supposed to give her. I will be blamed—not her father, not her friends and not this entire cultural context, which is far more tolerant and accommodating towards personal dietary preferences and requirements, particularly those of children, than Switzerland is.

KALE CHIPS

"Kale, kale! *Je veux du* kale! I want kale chips! Yummy for my tummy!" Fiona exclaims, fidgeting on her seat in the vegetable aisle. She is too big for it now, but she insists on riding in the cart while we shop at the discount grocery store close to our home. Other shoppers glance, amused. They probably rarely see a child enthusiastically asking for vegetables. I cannot afford the expensive, ready-made kale chips, so I buy a big bunch of kale, not organic, but locally produced in Ontario. In my own imperfect and mutable scale of values, this is better than buying imported produce.

While we prepare the chips together, I let her eat as many as she wants of the raw pieces, with just olive oil and salt, before the leaves go into the hot oven and turn into chips. On other days, this same child will refuse to eat even just one leaf of salad. I am confident that, in the end, her diet will be balanced. It would never cross my mind to precisely measure her intake of calories, fibers, and other nutriments. I do not like strategies to "trick" children into eating veggies by hiding them in "kids foods" such as macaroni. I follow another approach.

After almost three years in Canada, I have come to believe that picky eating is a cultural and cultivated phenomenon. Although it also exists in Switzerland, picky eating seems to be more prevalent in North America. Stating my opinion about this does not make it any easier to deal with. In their respective motherhood memoirs about their time spent in France as North American mothers, Pamela Druckerman and Karen LeBillon reach similar conclusions. Is picky eating a culturally transmitted disease? Is it curable? In the long run, it might have serious consequences for some children (though, fortunately, not the majority of them): a contemporary form of malnutrition—nutritional to some extent, but perhaps also cultural, as McDowell suggests, making the case against "kids menus" and "kids food" in an article aptly entitled "Death to the Chicken Finger." Society readily blames mothers instead of looking at a wider and more complex system of interactions, influences, and constraints, now dominated by agribusiness lobbies, gigantic food corporations, and marketing. Not having cable TV at home saves us, at least, from advertising for these foods. Chocolate bars and breakfast cereals, not vegetables, are packaged with Disney movies characters.

In their books, Druckerman and Le Billon uncover which resources "French parenting" has to offer in this matter. Most of the educative principles that they make explicit are just plain common sense to me, probably because I was raised according to very similar ones and in a cultural context close to that of France, though distinct from it by many aspects. Now that I am in a situation similar to that of the North American mothers addressed in these books, I feel that some of their advice simply cannot be applied. "Raising happy, healthy eaters" (Le Billon) is more difficult in an environment where snacking is not only tolerated, but also encouraged and where picky eating is regarded as normal, and short-order cooking for children is not uncommon. Taking into account and adapting to my parenting environment, I am bound to resort to resources played out mostly in my own privatized domestic sphere. I feel fortunate that I have at least one person on my side. The task would be much harder without having both parents on the same page regarding foodways.

Feeding and parenting our "new Canadian" daughter in Toronto is more of an everyday cultural challenge than a nutritional one. We never expected that the intersection of food and parenting would constitute an issue for us. Nevertheless, we are glad that it does. Our still ongoing experience in negotiating habits of two compatible but still very different cultural contexts has prompted us to redefine certain notions about our identity and values, as newcomers and as parents.

WORKS CITED

Druckerman, Pamela. *Bringing Up Bébé. One American Mother Discovers the Wisdom of French Parenting*. New York: The Penguin Press, 2012. Print.

Gopnik, Adam. *The Table Comes First: Family, France, and the Meaning of Food*. New York: Knopf, 2011. Print.

Le Billon, Karen. *French Kids Eat Everything {And Yours Can Too}: How Our Family Moved to France, Cured Picky Eating, Banned Snacking, and Discovered 10 Simple Rules for Raising Happy, Healthy Eaters*. Toronto: HarperCollins, 2012. Print.

Mannur, Anita. *Culinary Fictions: Food in South Asian Diasporic Culture*. Philadelphia: Temple University Press, 2010. Print.

McDowell, Adam. "Death to the Chicken Finger." *The National Post*. Web. 2 May 2015.

Parkhurst Ferguson, Priscilla. *Word of Mouth: What We Talk About When We Talk About Food*. Berkeley: University of California Press, 2014. Print.

Ruddick, Sara. *Maternal Thinking. Towards a Politics of Peace*. New York: Ballantine Books, 1989. Print.

14.
Wa and *Wa-shoku*

Mothering and Food as an American in Japan

WENDY JONES NAKANISHI

THE WORD *WA* IS THE OLDEST RECORDED NAME of Japan, and *wa-shoku* means Japanese cuisine. *Wa* also has the connotation of harmony or team spirit: a fundamental tenet in this ancient country. In the following, I discuss Japan and Japanese traditions about food from a personal perspective as an American resident in Japan for over thirty years.

Japan remains in thrall to the old tradition that the ideal to which its womenfolk should aspire is that of the "good wife, wise mother" or *ryōsai kenbo*: a self-sacrificing, submissive being who devotes her life to the care of her husband and children. This idealized figure first was popularized in legends and folklore in the late 1800s, but she dates back to Japan's distant past and continues to exert a potent force on Japanese social attitudes in the twenty-first century, despite the so-called emancipation of Japanese women following the country's defeat in the Second World War.

Although nearly half of Japanese women are in full-time work, they tend to be in low-paid positions, condemned, by virtue of their sex, to menial jobs. Despite working long hours and being expected to manage the household almost singlehandedly with their husbands away from early in the morning to late at night at their own jobs, Japanese women are still the keystone of the family. In Japan, that self-sacrificing figure of the idealized mother not only must provide her family with delicious, healthy food but also must act as the "main agent of [her] child's socialisation," with almost the full burden of the child's education and conduct falling on her shoulders (Kiefer 346). She is the lynchpin of the family unit. By custom, the husband is expected to turn over his salary to her, and she manages the household finances, doling out an allowance to him as though he were a child.

The ramifications of a Japanese marriage were unclear to me until I married a Japanese farmer over twenty-eight years ago. I soon learned that I was expected to shop every day; to be able to fillet the fresh fish one of our neighbours periodically brought by, courtesy of a husband who spent every weekend fishing; and to master a wide array of culinary techniques in preparing the fish or meat as well as the fruit and vegetables accompanying the rice and miso soup that form a component of most meals.

Upon having children, I was made to feel my culinary inadequacy on the occasion of the frequent outings or picnics arranged by their schools. The packed sandwiches and hard-boiled eggs that I made for my sons simply didn't measure up. On these mornings, the other mothers would rise at dawn to spend hours labouring over a boxed lunch that featured not only the obligatory serving of rice but also a wide and colourful array of fruit and vegetables, meat and fish fashioned into exquisite shapes. These were not simply lunches: they were works of art. The typical Japanese housewife is a skilled technician who can wield a knife with razor-thin precision. To tempt a fussy little eater, the bed of rice might be transformed into a happy face by an addition of curled shavings of celery as eyebrows and eyes, a pickled plum for a nose, and a smiling sliver of carrot serving as a mouth. Little sausages might be carved to resemble cute puppies. With a few deft slices of a knife, three or four cherry tomatoes could be made to look like a bouquet of blushing dahlias, or a piece of cucumber, like an octopus propelled along by its tentacles.

The preparation of traditional Japanese food is a labour-intensive process. Japanese cuisine is expected to appeal to the eye equally as to the palate. The Japanese dislike of flavoured dishes touching each other means that a great deal of crockery is used for any meal. Each dish is in its *own* dish. This fact, coupled with the rarity of the dishwasher in the Japanese kitchen, means that clearing up after each meal requires time and effort.

In the first years of our marriage, my Japanese husband Takehito was dismayed by what he perceived as my bad food habits and balked at pandering to them. Despite what he agreed was revoltingly bland hospital food, he refused, for example, to bring me McDonald's takeaway on the three occasions that I spent a week recuperating in hospital after the birth of our sons. He ascribed my occasional longing for junk food to my being an American. As a Japanese, he was raised in a far different way than I had been and had quite different ideas about food.

I first arrived in Japan many years ago to take up a position teaching English at a small private university. Upon marrying and then becoming pregnant, I learned that it was not considered seemly for me to continue to live as a foreigner, regarding Japanese customs with a detached eye. I was expected not only to assimilate into Japanese culture but also to strive to emulate Japanese women with children in aiming to become a perfect mother. It was no surprise to me when I learned that the idealization of the mother as the bedrock of Japanese society has been likened to a religious faith (Ohinata 205). I have become an adherent, inculcated in the values of this faith, because I am settled in a part of the country where old traditions hold sway, and I have married a farmer who lives in close proximity to his family.

Japan consists of four main islands and innumerable tiny ones. We live on the smallest, most rural of the four: Shikoku. Takehito belongs to a family that, like five or six neighbouring families, has farmed this area of gentle slopes covered by fruit trees and rice paddies for hundreds of years. He grew up in an old traditional Japanese farmhouse constructed a century ago. It is a black, squat, two-story building stooping under a heavy tiled roof. It sits between two storehouses in a dusty courtyard enclosed by high stone walls: the family compound. Few rooms inside the farmhouse have fixed walls and some contain scarcely any furniture. Sliding panels can be added or removed to make larger or smaller spaces as the occasion or necessity requires.

Takehito recalls that the kitchen of his childhood had a hard dirt floor. His mother and his father's mother, who lived with them, discarded vegetable and fruit peelings on the floor as they cooked, to be swept up later. There was no refrigerator or stove, and electrical equipment was limited to a single light bulb dangling from the ceiling. His mother and grandmother cooked over a wood-burning brazier. Takehito fondly describes the kitchen as a dark, smoky place. As a little boy, he was expected to sweep its dirt floor and to collect twigs and branches from the forested mountainsides for the kitchen fire and for the fire that would heat the family bath.

Takehito's descriptions of his childhood remind me of my mother's. She also grew up in a farming family, but one located in the American Midwest. She and her parents and older sister occupied a farm of three hundred acres in central Indiana. My grandfather raised cattle and pigs, cultivated fields of tomatoes for a nearby ketchup factory, and also grew feed crops such as corn and wheat. Like Takehito's mother, my grandmother kept poultry both for the eggs and for the occasional treat of a chicken dinner.

For Takehito and his parents and for my mother and hers, life was hard. There were privations and difficulties. They relied on kerosene lamps, with only three or four electric lights in the house. There were no flush toilets. Any water to be used for cooking or baths had to be pumped by hand. My mother's mother, like Takehito's mother in Japan, cooked with fire, although my grandmother was not limited to a small brazier. She prepared her elaborate meals on a big iron wood-burning stove that constantly needed to be replenished with logs taken from a woodshed located just outside.

On the other hand, there were advantages to this seemingly primitive existence. I used to feel envious hearing my husband and my mother reminisce about their childhood experiences. While I had an intimate acquaintance with so-called TV dinners and with canned or frozen food from my earliest years, they had meals constituted from genuine, unadulterated ingredients, prepared with ingenuity and skill. My mother recalls her own mother chasing after hens in the farmyard to kill and pluck them for her famed chicken and dumpling dinners. Takehito remembers his grandmother pickling vegetables and the old woman who trundled a trolley to their house every morning, for his mother to make her selection of the day's catch of fresh fish. Vegetables and fruit were all home grown.

After my long residence in this country, I have come to conclude that the best of Japanese cookery represents a triumph of making a virtue of necessity. With no gas or electric stoves at their disposal, former generations of Japanese perfected the art of grilling and roasting meat and fish, of stewing vegetables over a low flame, and of preparing exquisite platters of raw fish and vegetables. With no refrigerators or freezers to store food, they became adept at pickling a wide variety of vegetables to complement the daily fare of rice. Sweets were provided in the form of dried fruit; in autumn, it is still not uncommon to see a line of dried persimmons strung out like a festive line of yellow ornaments on the porch of a Japanese farmhouse.

In America, my siblings and I grew up with plenty and were free to wander the aisles of well-stocked grocery stores that offered anything we might long for. The problem was convincing our mother to buy raw ingredients and to cook them for us as opposed to heating up a ready-made meal in the oven. It was a far different situation in Japan in the 1950s, when there was still scarcity of food and actual privation. My husband talks of having had to share a single egg with his brother at breakfast when they were children: the rest of the eggs provided by the family's poultry had to be sold.

But he enjoyed advantages that I could only dream of. My acquaintance with fish as a child was limited to canned tuna and sardines while Takehito was offered a huge range of fresh seafood. Like all Japanese, he is adept at de-boning a fish with a few deft movements of his chopsticks. His favourite is Pacific saury, a long, thin silvery fish—its beady black eyes staring sightlessly from the head and its finny tail intact—served whole with a drizzling of soy sauce and a mound of grated *daikon*, giant Japanese radish, on the side. For my husband, it is a special treat, and he insists on preparing it himself, broiling one for each of us. While I labour over mine and sometimes must resort to a knife and fork, Takehito dispatches his quickly and efficiently, leaving a cleanly picked skeleton on his plate. I prefer the buttery sweet flesh of yellowtail; my children like smoky mackerel, its strong flavour undercut by ginger slices, while my mother-in-law often presents us with one of her specialties: turbot stewed in fish stock.

Naturally, my husband, a farmer, has always advocated the use of the freshest ingredients possible. Takehito grows mandarin oranges, tangerines, limes, and a large, fleshy, thick-skinned fruit, resembling a grapefruit, called *dekopon* that I have never seen outside Japan. He used to grow hothouse Muscat grapes. He and his mother maintain a large vegetable garden that supplies us with cucumbers, okra, tomatoes, potatoes, onions, leeks, lettuce, and daikon. Takehito occasionally grows strawberries for us in a corner of one of his greenhouses, and a long line of fig trees borders the orange grove. Our neighbours, farmers themselves, present us with gifts of kiwi fruit, loquats, and persimmons that they grow.

Visitors to Japan often comment on the prominent role food plays in this culture. Japanese television broadcasts many cooking programs as well as shows featuring young, attractive girls travelling about the country and sampling regional culinary delights. There is a kind of reverence for food in Japan, attributable both to its native religion, Shinto, which perceives the presence of god in all of nature, as well as to the widespread starvation during and following the Second World War.

There is also a strength of tradition and uniformity of cultural practices in Japan that, as an American, I find surprising. It has often been said that the Japanese resemble a tribe or an extended family rather than a nation made up of many disparate individuals. It is a homogenous society, with only roughly one percent of the population hailing from other lands. There is an emphasis on self-discipline, an adherence to old rules about gender differences, and a belief in putting the needs of the group—whether that group is the family unit or the workers at a company or the Japanese nation itself—above those of the individual: the group needs to work together in harmony or *wa*. The food customs, including woman's perceived "natural" role in the household that I have described above, are common throughout Japan and have been for centuries.

We live, according to Japanese custom, a short distance from Takehito's mother (his father passed away several years ago). The family is of great importance in the Japanese social structure, and my mother-in-law, or *Okaasan*, as I am supposed to call her, has played an important role in our lives. If I had been a Japanese wife, my husband and I would have lived with my in-laws after our marriage, and I would have been expected to quit my job upon having children to concentrate on raising them properly. In Japan, even in the twenty-first century, motherhood is often considered to be a profession "incompatible with a career" (Jolivet 45).

As a foreigner and, unusually, as the family's principal bread-winner, I was exempted from this general pattern. But this meant I had to rely heavily on *Okaasan*. I needed to return to my full-time job, teaching at a private university, three months after the birth of each baby. Until each boy reached his first birthday, when he could be enrolled in the local nursery school, he had to be entrusted to the care of *Okaasan*. My mother-in-law is very much of the traditional school. She advocated cloth rather than paper diapers, and there was no question of her using store-bought baby food. I would return home from work to find *Okaasan* preparing healthy home-made concoctions for my boys. Soft rice flavoured with fish stock and seaweed figured prominently in these meals, accompanied by tiny, diced carrots and potatoes and, occasionally, small dried fish.

I think my sons have been very fortunate in spending their childhood in Japan. It has meant that they have eaten well and learned a proper respect for food and for those who prepare it. The lunches provided by the nursery schools and kindergartens, by the elementary and the junior high schools, for example, are of an exceptionally high nutritional standard and, I can confirm from personal experience, very tasty. To my chagrin, when they were little, my children occasionally asked me why I couldn't cook such wonderful meals as those they had at school.

In Japanese primary and junior high schools, the children play an instrumental role in serving *kyu-shoku*, or school lunches, from the age of six until fifteen, and all are expected to follow a strict ritual in its consumption. Personal hygiene is stressed, particularly in the early years. In primary school, the students don white caps that cover their hair, face masks for their noses and mouths, and white aprons like long cloaks over their school uniforms. They carefully wash their hands with soap and water. Those children appointed as the day's monitors go to the refectory to collect the lunch. They bring containers of food as well as trays, chopsticks, dishes and cups back to the classroom, where they will dole out portions for each child and for the teacher. Junior high school students are allowed to dispense with the caps, masks and aprons, but the process is otherwise the same. According to Japanese custom, all wait until everyone has been served, and then, in unison, they bow to the food set out on the tray on their desks and clap their hands together while saying *itadakimasu* or "We gratefully receive this offering." When everyone has eaten their fill, the same procedure is followed with the words *gochisoosamadeshita*, or "We give thanks for this food," concluding the meal as the children hold up steepled hands as if in prayer. The monitors then collect all the dishes and trays and pots and pans to carry back to the school kitchen to be washed by the cooks.

The ingredients are locally sourced and prepared, but the typical menu is the same throughout the country. There is always a small bottle of milk and a bowl of hot steaming white rice. There is usually some kind of soup or stew. There are vegetables—stewed or boiled or served as a salad—and fish or meat and a piece of fresh fruit. On special occasions, one of my favourite dishes might be featured: a savoury steamed egg custard with shrimp, mushrooms, and a gingko nut inside.

But not only Japanese food is on offer; there is also spaghetti and pizza and curry, salads and soups and rolls, all freshly prepared each day at each school. A menu of the month's meals including pictures of each day's offering is sent home with each child. Our youngest boy, the most interested in food, used to enjoy poring over these menus, anticipating his favourite dishes.

Like my mother, I am not a particularly skilled let alone an inspired cook. The difference between us is that I derive a sense of fulfillment from doing household chores that always eluded her. I came to Japan as an American, believing in rights that I could exercise as an individual, impatient of having demands made on me. Living in a society that frowns on self-gratification and promotes restraint and social harmony has represented a difficult education. There have been tears and tantrums, the stamping of feet and the slamming of doors. But long residence in this country has resulted in my coming to subscribe to elements of that traditional Japanese ideal of the *ryōsai kenbo* that I mentioned at the beginning of this paper.

Although Japanese women remain, to an extent, second-class citizens in their own country, I am fortunate enough to have been able to combine having a well-paid, highly-respected career with having a family. As I've noted, the old Japanese ideal of woman was of a being both submissive and self-sacrificing. My position at a Japanese university means that people—my students, at least—tend to obey *me*. I need not be submissive, but I recognize that self-sacrifice is a necessary component of my role as wife and mother. *Self-sacrifice* is one of those paradoxical terms that can mean in practice the opposite of what it implies: it *is* more blessed to give than it is to receive, and personal experience has confirmed to me that whatever we do to help others, we get back in abundance.

My "self sacrifice" includes my willingness to expend the time and effort to prepare the best food possible for my family. My repertoire combines Japanese and western cuisine. As for the latter, I indulge food preferences inherited from my Indiana childhood by baking casseroles and making pots of chilli and vegetable soup and, when my boys were small, popping popcorn every Friday night. I also have always cooked ethnic dishes, as I wanted my boys to experience something of the world's wonderful variety of food. I am well aware that I represent an object of curiosity to my neighbours and relatives here, who seem to invent pretexts to drop by at mealtimes to find out what the local foreigner provides her family and how she serves it to them. I know my practices are gratifyingly odd to them on both counts.

I am averse to extremism. Although I have come increasingly to dislike fast food, I was raised on it and am fully aware of its attractions. When they were little, my boys and I reached a happy compromise. I would buy them soft drinks once every two or three weeks and occasionally take them to a McDonald's in the neighbourhood. Making clear my own disinclination to eat such food, I would sit in the car waiting for them. They would emerge looking satiated, content, and slightly guilty.

Now that they are adults and require neither my permission nor my assistance in frequenting places like McDonald's, I am relieved to find they all seem to prefer home-cooked meals and scarcely ever visit fast food joints. But I worry about their future, when my boys leave home. In adopting the role of the traditional Japanese wife and mother, I have always managed nearly all the cooking and most of the housework. As the proverb says, "the road to hell is paved with good intentions." On the few occasions when my sons have needed to prepare their own lunch or dinner, I have returned home to find empty polystyrene containers of "Pot Noodles" littering the kitchen table.

Increasingly, I try to have the two sons still at home do household chores so that they can manage on their own and, one day, become reliable and useful husbands and fathers. Even in Japan, change is making itself felt. Twenty-first-century Japan is witnessing the gradual breaking down of the traditional gender roles. When I first began working at a Japanese university thirty years ago, I found to my dismay that all my female colleagues were single. They told me that the weight of custom meant that they had felt they needed to make a choice: a career or a family. Now my college's teaching staff has many women who are wives and mothers, and it is even possible these days to see young men shopping for groceries with young children, a sight inconceivable even fifteen years ago.

My sons belong to Japan in a way that I never could, whether I wished to or not. They love it here and lament the inaccessibility of Japanese food whenever we venture to other countries. I sometimes grieve that my boys can never really know my own childhood culture and that, in a sense, as a *gaijin*, or foreigner, in Japan, I am reduced always to the role of an onlooker here.

But, despite their love of this country, my children may not live in Japan forever. We inhabit a restless, mobile age. My Japanese husband worked in Africa for three years, and I have lived for extended periods in Britain, Holland, France, and now Japan. But wherever my boys end up, I imagine that they will remember the food of their childhood: its odd mixture of the cuisine of Indiana and Japan, with an occasional flavouring of the ethnic foods that I made when they were little. I hope it will always be a good memory for them and that, when the time comes, I will have prepared them to make their own forays into the world, receptive to its banquet of culinary delights.

WORKS CITED

Jolivet, Muriel. *Japan: The Childless Society? The Crisis of Motherhood*. London: Routledge, 1997. Print.

Kiefer, Christie W. "The Psychological Interdependence of Family, School and Bureaucracy in Japan." *Japanese Culture and Behavior: Selected Readings*. Ed. Takie Sugiyama Lebra and William P. Lebra. Honolulu: the University Press of Hawaii, 1974. 342-356. Print.

Ohinata, Masami. "The Mystique of Motherhood: A Key to Understanding Social Change and Family Problems in Japan." *Japanese Women: New Feminist Perspectives on the Past, Present and Future*. Ed. Kumiko Fujimura-Faneslow and Atsuko Kamada. New York: The Feminist Press, 1995. 199-212. Print.

15.
The Rebellious Bento Box

Slapdash Western Mothering in Perfectionist Japan

MEREDITH STEPHENS

WESTERN MOTHERS OFTEN DOCUMENT childrearing in Japan as an anthropological exercise (Benjamin; Allison), but the practice of a Western mother rearing her children in Japan as an educational choice is uncommon. This is an account of my experience as an observer and participant in the context of mothering and food, not as an anthropologist but as a mother who happened to be working in a remote part of Japan. Our town was far from international schools, but it did not matter as I wanted a Japanese education for my children. This is a story of how despite good intentions, I could not overcome my slapdash approach to preparing food for my children. Nevertheless, it did not prevent my children from thriving.

First, I should explain how my upbringing made me particularly unsuited to the role of a mother in Japan. I had been raised in a household where discussions of Betty Friedan and Germaine Greer were common, and not once can I remember having been instructed in the culinary arts. All that mattered when growing up were discussions of writers and current events, and of course other people's life events. Those concerning domestic matters were rare. Being preoccupied with serious ideas was the norm, and my family culture taught me to scorn "trivial" topics, such as household chores.

My first daughter, Elizabeth, was born in the appropriately named Queen Elizabeth Hospital in Australia. She was unwillingly summoned into this world because of maternal pre-eclampsia. After a failed induction, Elizabeth was pulled out in haste in an emergency

Caesarean section. She was the most distressed baby on the ward, and even the most experienced nurses had trouble helping her to stop crying. Meanwhile, because my breast milk had not come in, due to the Caesarean section, I was unable to feed her. Still, the nurses insisted breast was best and saw no need to give in to the formula alternative. Days later, and after much patience, my breast milk came in, and Elizabeth learned to suckle. We mapped her growth onto the height and weight chart and were relieved to see that she was thriving.

When Elizabeth was seven weeks old, the doctors gave us permission to travel, and we boarded the plane to Japan to meet Elizabeth's dad whose journey had preceded ours. It was a daunting experience to be in a foreign country with a newborn baby, with no relatives, apart from my husband, no car, and no income of my own. Admittedly, I was somewhat familiar with Japan as I had studied there for several years on two occasions. I was on unpaid childrearing leave from my teaching position in Australia, with possible extensions until my (yet unborn) youngest child reached school age. I wanted to use this opportunity to spend more time in Japan and had therefore urged my husband, Roland, to start a new career there. This choice presented unanticipated difficulties. Suddenly deprived of an income, I had a completely helpless human being dependent on me twenty-four hours a day. At least Elizabeth had learned to breastfeed so that I could feed her whenever and wherever I wanted. Elizabeth's need to feed overrode any concerns of the appropriateness of the time, place, or occasion, and she continued to thrive.

The local community health centre in the city of Takasago, was offering free checks for babies, so I took Elizabeth along to be weighed and measured. After weighing Elizabeth, the nurse scolded me because she was underweight. She attributed this to the inadequacy of my milk, and urged me to supplement it with formula.

She gave me the growth chart to confirm her accusations. I was dumbfounded. After all the effort and encouragement to become a proficient breast feeder in Australia, I was being told my baby was failing to thrive. I went home in distress and compared the Australian and Japanese growth charts. I was vindicated; the growth charts were different. The Australian ones accepted a lower weight relative to height than the Japanese one did: it was acceptable to have a lower weight for breastfed babies.

Once Elizabeth was able to take solids, I had to feed her according to local customs for baby food. On the advice of Japanese friends, I boiled rice until it became a thick soup, known as *okayu*, and Elizabeth quickly put on weight with this delicious addition to her diet. A highly strung child, Elizabeth managed to sleep through the Great Hanshin earthquake, even when the apartment was shuddering around her, and continued to adequately put on weight, even by Japanese standards. "Carry them small before they are born, and raise them to be big babies after birth," a friend had advised me. I was no longer chided for having an underweight child.

Elizabeth continued to grow and thrive, and three years later Annabel popped into the world to join her. Conceived in Madrid, spending most of her time in utero in Japan, and born in Australia, this child had an embarrassment of cross-cultural experience even before she had even made her entrance from the womb. Again, I became a proud breast feeder of a sometimes unwilling Annabel, even when the only time she would accept breast milk was when she was asleep. When Annabel was a year old, Roland once again secured a contract in Japan. I obtained an extension to my childrearing leave, and we set off for another stint of childrearing in a foreign land.

KINDERGARTEN

I had assumed that my shortcomings regarding nourishing my children were over now that we had survived babyhood, but this was only the beginning. Providing an acceptable *obento* lunchbox at kindergarten presented an insurmountable challenge. Describing the Japanese attitude to mothers providing food, Allison explains: "Food may not be casual ... nor the producer casual in her production. In those two rules is a message both about social order and the role gender plays in sustaining and nourishing that order" (158).

Even as an outsider, I was expected to conform to these rules. My role as a mother overruled my identity as a foreigner. The mother of Elizabeth's kindergarten friend advised me: "You need to include the colours red, yellow, and green in the *obento*. Then you can decorate the rice balls with cut-outs of animation characters in seaweed." She gave me a packet of seaweed cut-outs of animation characters, and a packet of aluminum cases, which resembled cupcake containers, to present the individual items in the *obento*. These were inserted into a tiny, sometimes two-tiered lunchbox, secured with a special band, and then inserted into a drawstring bag decorated with animation characters. Some mothers had the audacity to buy sets of tiny frozen serves for the *obento* to make it look as if they had risen early to concoct these healthy delicacies. I soon joined their ranks by inserting into the *obento* mini serves of *hijiki* seaweed, delectable spinach and sweet corn, *ohitashi*, and julienned burdock known as *kinpira gobo*. The appeal of these frozen serves was that they would thaw at room temperature, so you could just insert them delicately into the *obento* and then they would be ready to eat at lunchtime. I used this convenient strategy until my children tired of the frozen serves.

It was not just the other mothers who gave me advice. The principal of the kindergarten advised me "*kokoro o komete*," which implies that the act of making lunch for my child was an expression of maternal love. That was a novel thought, but I interpreted it as emotional blackmail. I had never imagined proving my worth as a mother by the care that I put into providing lunch. The Western side of me considered that the other expressions of commitment such as reading books together, talking, answering questions, and playing together were just as important. Still, this perceived need to physically demonstrate my worth as a mother by providing a beautiful and nutritious *obento* added to my sense of inadequacy.

Three years of kindergarten provided a long-term challenge in terms of providing *obento*, to which my slapdash approach was not suited. Having no preconceived notions of what the prescribed colours of red, yellow and green should represent, I started inserting fresh kiwi slices to represent the green slot. To my great surprise, I was chided by the kindergarten teacher: "Annabel has too much fruit. You are not supposed to put fruit in the *obento*."

I realized later that dessert might come in the form of a single grape, but not large slices of kiwi. However, vindication came when the local television crew visited the kindergarten in their rounds of all of the local kindergartens. Annabel was featured on television eating her slice of kiwi with chopsticks, accompanied by flattering music which resembled the *Nutcracker Suite*. Perhaps they had chosen to film Annabel because it was so unusual to see large slices of kiwi in an *obento* eaten by a child from another country, but the accompanying music was so endearing that I couldn't help but feel a sense of pride.

Nevertheless, my attitude towards the task of making *obentos* continued to be flippant. I did my best to hide this casual attitude from my Japanese peers out of respect for their feelings and traditions. Deep down I was in agreement with Seddon who writes that "bento is not only a stifling chore, but symbolic of a larger social problem of female subordination" (306).

ELEMENTARY AND MIDDLE SCHOOL

Even after I had survived being a parent of kindergarteners in Japan, my fascination with educating my children there had not subsided, and I left my Australian employer to work in the local Japanese university. The most welcome aspect of the transition to a being a parent of children in an elementary school and then middle school was the knowledge that school lunches would be provided, and I would be spared the agony of the constant criticism of my *obentos*. The quality of each meal was taken just as seriously, but it was no longer I who had to provide it. The school provided us with a monthly menu in advance. It included a table of the carbohydrates, proteins, vegetables, and calorie counts of each meal. The sourcing of the dish featured each month was also explained. For both Elizabeth and Annabel, the school lunch was the highlight of each day. Elizabeth used to say that she looked forward to lunch all morning, and then she looked forward to going home all afternoon. Annabel developed such a strong preference for Japanese food, thanks to the school lunch, that her teachers would comment about how she would lose weight whenever she returned from a trip to Australia.

However Annabel did not take to eating plain rice, and on her first day of school, she did not touch it. Even before picking her up from school that day, I heard independently from three people that Annabel had not finished her rice. Clearly the quality of my *obento* had not been the only reason for the attention that Annabel received. People were actually interested in what kind of food that she did and didn't like.

Both children developed a preference for Japanese food. They would pester me at the supermarket to buy exotic delicacies such as *natto* (fermented beans), sesame salad dressing, dried seaweed for soup, *iriko* (tiny dried fish with heads and eyes intact), and packets of dried octopi and squid for after school snacks. As a curvy westerner who had been brought up on yeast buns and cakes, I would instead offer to buy them some chocolate biscuits, but to no avail.

Not only did the food present a challenge, but so did the complicated rituals surrounding the event of school lunch. Children had to cover their desk with a white tablecloth at every lunch. This cloth was brought home every Friday to be washed over the weekend. Strict instructions were provided to parents concerning how to iron creases into the right places of the tablecloth. In addition to the tablecloth, the apron, chef's hat, and mask would come home to be washed once a month. Children were rotated on lunch duty each day. They had to go to the school kitchen and bring the lunch to the classroom where it was served. When it was my children's turn to serve lunch, it was my turn to wash the apron, hat, and mask over the weekend.

The most troubling dish served to Annabel was whale meat. At the time, Australia and Japan were in conflict about whaling in Antarctica. Now whale meat appeared in the monthly menu. It was not a staple dish, so it was only served once or twice a year. Annabel said that it was fatty and not particularly tasty. A Japanese friend casually apologized to me for serving whale meat at school when my country was so opposed to whaling.

HIGH SCHOOL

The maternal bliss stemming from nine years of school lunches came to an end at the beginning of senior high school. Children had to either bring their lunches or buy their lunch at the school cafeteria. Rumour had it that because of the *sempai kohai* relationship—privileges given to older children over newcomers—it was hard for first year students to get served in the cafeteria. This left no option other than once again providing *obento*. However, after my countless failures at providing an adequate *obento*, I no longer had the desire to prove myself as a Japanese homemaker. As long as my children had something filling and nutritious, it didn't matter if it wasn't a work of art. Still, I was naive to think that just because my children were now in high school, people would no longer take interest in the kind of lunch their mother provided.

Japanese *obento* commonly consists of cooked vegetables which have been allowed to cool, such as cold broccoli, sliced lotus root, and julienned burdock. However, I was in the habit of serving these kinds of vegetables hot; serving them cold would be anathema as would be serving cold rice. Instead, I packed Elizabeth's lunchbox with raw vegetables, such as salad vegetables, and then her friend teased her by calling her a horse. Other friends felt sorry for her because she had a mum with such inferior *obento* skills. They then started donating food to her from their *obentos*. By this time, I no longer had the close-knit associations with other mothers that I had had when she was in kindergarten, and so I felt free from peer pressure to conform to the local maternal ideal. I was now more confident in my own cultural ideal of motherhood and assigned less importance to food preparation.

When Annabel's turn came to start high school, all I wanted for her was to have a filling and nutritious, if not well-balanced, lunch. I stopped packing items that came back untouched, and eventually I ended up just packing items that she did in fact eat, such as grapes and strawberries. She wouldn't eat the staple of cold rice that the other children brought, and she refused to eat bread. Her teacher worried that she was not eating enough and discussed this concern with me at the parent-teacher interview. I was well past the limits for humiliation and instead was happy that someone else cared enough for her welfare. Annabel herself realized how unusual her lunches were and uploaded a photo of her *obento* on social media. Now my *obento* making skills had gone viral, and I received comments from a Japanese friend in a distant city.

MY CULINARY SKILLS

My Japanese friends would enthusiastically try to share with me simple dishes that they thought I could master. Fried rice proved surprisingly easy and a good way to use up leftover rice. I became adept at making *onigiri* rice balls; I cupped them in my hand to form a triangle, inserted an *umeboshi* sour plum, and then wrapped them in seaweed. My *onigiri* even proved popular with the neighbourhood children. This was a considerable feat because it was hard to make Japanese food for discerning Japanese palates. Other friends enthusiastically taught me how to make *sukiyaki*—thin slices of beef, and vegetables, cooked in a broth, and then dipped in raw egg. A friend bought my daughter a special rectangular shaped frypan to make *tamagoyaki*, an egg roll that could be sliced and inserted into the *obento*. Others taught me how to make *okonomiyaki* vegetable pancakes topped with slivers of seaweed and dried bonito flakes. Another inspired me to make ramen with spinach, bean sprouts, and thinly sliced pork. Even my hairdresser cajoled me into making *ohitashi* spinach and sweet corn dishes, insisting it was easy, and in fact, it was. Their sheer enthusiasm left me ashamed of my lack of commitment. I had never had such conversations in English. Cooking had been banished as a topic of conversation for English-speaking women of my subculture within Japanese society. It was not my intention to introduce contemporary Western culture to my Japanese friends. Instead, I was there to learn, and cooking for your children was a major conversation topic among Japanese mothers. Allison explains that there is more to women's labour in making *obento* than simply having children finish their lunch. She argues that this food preparation indicates their commitment to childrearing and to their identity, "a representation and a product of the woman herself" (165). Accordingly, my Japanese friends' enthusiasm for sharing their culinary skills with me was a way of connecting with me; they were sharing with me important parts of their identity, which, in this particular culture, happened to be creative, elaborate, and delicious forms of food preparation.

BALANCE AND VARIETY

As if the "meat and three veg" rule in Australia hadn't been enough, in Japan we were urged to consume thirty-three different elements of food every day. This was clearly not the level of variety that I had been used to. We were living in Ehime on the island of Shikoku, where some people say that they produce the most delicious mandarins in the world. In winter, I noticed the most common greeting was "Do you have any mandarins?" Everyone seemed to have friends with an orchard and was receiving more bags of mandarins than they could possibly consume. People's fingers turned orange from peeling mandarins, and the rest of their skin turned orange from the consumption of mandarins. Being no stranger to excess, I failed to urge restraint on my children, and went even further than the locals in my pursuit of orange skin. Rather than the standard rice, miso soup, fish and salad, Annabel would consume six mandarins for breakfast. Nevertheless, the lack of variety didn't seem to stop her from continuing to be the tallest girl in the class.

Restraint was urged in the adage *hara hachi bu*, or "Stop eating when you are 80 percent full." I wish that I had grown up with this wisdom. If my experience growing up had been summarized, it would have been "Eat until you are 120 percent full," a quick route to poor health. Thankfully both girls, but particularly Elizabeth, managed to apply this ancient Japanese wisdom, even after their return to the excesses of Western culinary culture. Needless to say, their mother has not outgrown her Western habits, and we are in the unusual situation where the children demonstrate more restraint than their mother.

ELIZABETH AND ANNABEL'S GROWTH

Despite having difficulty breastfeeding and receiving poor high school *obento*, Elizabeth and Annabel continued to top the class in height in the triennial health checks. It must have been at least partly due to the nutritious school lunches. Before they were adolescents, I was used to being perceived as a mother with her children. They continued grow in height to such a degree that in our annual sojourns to Australia we were no longer treated as a mother and her children. Clerks would expect that we would pay separately at the cash register. At the time, I thought that that was because we were in a country where we looked like the majority of other people and could not be identified as a family. To my great consternation, this started happening in Japan too. When we would go out to restaurants, it would alarm me to be asked if we were paying together. I started buying higher heels in order to catch up with them, but to no avail. This was only reassuring in the sense that, despite my culinary failings, they continued to spurt.

CONCLUSIONS

You may ask why a modern mother raised in Australia would take norms from another culture so seriously. Why would I allow the principal of a kindergarten to chide me by saying that a mother's love can be expressed through the lunch that she makes for her child? Preparing food for my children in Japan was challenging for me but good for their health. They continue to have healthier preferences than I do. I indulge in a high-fat, high-sugar diet, and they spurn these choices, instead preferring to buy Japanese food whenever they can. I even extend my mothering preferences to our dogs, and I offer them pieces of toast, pasta, and chocolate cake. But Elizabeth and Annabel scold me, and they insist that the dogs have rice with their kangaroo mince. I had a radically different model of a woman's role in Australia. I was absorbing rules from my Japanese peers that were counter to those I had been raised with. The notion of a mother expressing her love through the practice of providing nourishment had simply never occurred to me. I was too obstinate to ever become converted to this idea, but I could certainly respect it in others. My children thrived despite my culinary inadequacies. If you ask them what part of Japanese culture that they miss most after our relocation to Australia, they will tell you, of course, it's the food.

ENDNOTE

[1]Pseudonyms have been used for the family members.

WORKS CITED

Allison, A. "Japanese Mothers and *Obentōs*: The Lunchbox as Ideological State Apparatus." *Food and Culture: A Reader. Third Edition.* Eds. Carole Counihan and Penny Van Esterik. New York: Taylor and Francis, 2013. 154-172. Print.

Benjamin, Gail R. *Japanese Lessons: A Year in a Japanese School through the Eyes of an American Anthropologist and Her Children.* New York: NYU Press, 1998. Print.

Seddon, Kiara. "Bento Blogs: Japanese Women's Expression in Digital Food Culture." *Women & Performance: A Journal of Feminist Theory* 21.3 (2011): 301-319. Web. 29 April 2015.

16.
An Ethnographic Analysis of U.S. Culture and Carribean Food Practices

ROSA E. SOTO AND SHARMILA PIXY FERRIS

WE ARE FIRST AND SECOND GENERATION immigrants to the United States: Rosa is a second generation Latina immigrant, and Pixy is a first generation Asian immigrant. Rosa was born in the U.S., but her family is from Puerto Rico and her upbringing was grounded in Puerto Rican food and culture. Pixy is from Mangalore, India, a small community with unique cultural traditions coming from an older Portuguese colonial culture.

This project started in the summer of 2013 when the two of us began to discuss the idea of food in immigrant communities. That summer, Rosa had visited her childhood home in Miami. An elaborate family meal, cooked by her mother and her mother's cousin (Esperanza) included a variety of traditional Puerto Rican dishes—*alcapurria, bacalaito, sorullos, bacalao con sebollas, chayote*, green bananas with batata—all delicious foods, but high in starch and fats. Rosa enjoyed the family time and the meal with all the accompanying storytelling, but she was very aware of the contents of the meal. Struggling with weight issues, Rosa very rarely ate meals like that in her everyday life in New Jersey, where she is surrounded by friends who are health-invested vegetarians or vegans, and organic food eaters. Pixy is just such a vegetarian and organic food eater! However, Pixy's traditional family celebrations follow a similar pattern to Rosa's, involving time-consuming and elaborately prepared family-centered meals, much higher in fat and starch than the norm.

Our conversations about food and culture were grounded in personal interest but had academic applications; Pixy recently had created a new General Education course about food as a lens for examining cultural, social, political and economic issues, and Rosa examined food as a regular discourse within her Latino Cultural Studies class. That year, the two of us organized several on-campus food events within ethnic communities. We heard from many students and faculty about issues related to traditional eating patterns in immigrant communities, including health issues that have been the focus of academic interest of late (Gerchow et. al 182-193). Our course-based and campus-wide conversations led to our increased interest in examining how food practices affect the identity of women when they immigrate to the U.S. We wondered: is anything lost in the practice of collecting, preparing, and learning to cook as mothers migrate? What elements, if any, of an ethnic reality are lost for individuals when such traditional cultural food practices are seen as not part of an Americanized identity? As we discussed these issues, we realized that although some texts certainly did examine the food of particular ethnic regions, our particular question of interest remained unexplored and warranted further exploration. In this chapter, we make a start at examining the "changes wrought by immigration in the deep structures of everyday life, especially in the realm of food practices" (Ray 4). We decided to focus our initial study of food practices on Latina women immigrants to the U.S.

IMMIGRANT FOOD PRACTICES IN THE UNITED STATES

The issue of migrant food practice has become increasingly important and has received growing attention, as the recent large NYU university study of obesity and health issues in Latina communities (Gerchow et al. 182-193) and other similar studies (Dillon, De La Rosa, and Ibanez 484-491; Yeh et al. 101-115) can attest. That the issue is moving beyond academe was brought home to us by the focus of a recent conference "Is Our Culture Killing Us?" led by healthy-lifestyle expert Maripili Rodriguez and moderator Yesi Morillo-Gual, a Dominican immigrant to the U.S., and president and founder of Proud to Be a Latina LLC. The conference examined the food choices that Latinas made in the U.S. that often led to high rates of obesity, heart disease, and diabetes. There was much discussion on the food divide between mothers and daughters. Daughters, often first-generation Latina Americans, are changing food patterns to reflect a sense of health consciousness and acculturation to the U.S., while their mothers' concerns are related to cooking traditional foods with connections to their home culture. This tension between mothers and daughters can lead to oppositional attitudes towards foods in these households and occasionally strained relationships between mothers and daughters. The conference chair noted strong connections between the roles of immigrant mothers and the importance of food in the mothering role.

Agreeing with Ms. Rodriguez (Rodriguez and Morillo-Gual) we feel that changes in Latina food habits have the potential to estrange us from our parents, and perhaps estrange us from our ethnic selves (Liu and Lianlian 135-162; Ray 94-98).

Although the issue of dual identity faces many groups—not just immigrants but, for example, people facing issues of ethnic identity and sexual orientation, among others—we as immigrant women feel a particular focus on different perceptions of food and foodways is important. Our own battle with dual ethnic identities and foodways is shared by many immigrant women (Lee 1-32; Zaman 43-44). From the perspective of this study, an examination of Latino foodways assumes special importance, given that Latinas/os are the largest immigrant group in the U.S., that one-third of Latinos are obese, and that they are 1.2 times more likely to be obese compared to non-Hispanic whites (Gerchow et al. 182-193).

Our personal experiences (Rosa's within a Caribbean-American immigrant family, and Pixy's within an Indian-American immigrant family) are reflective of many immigrant mothers and daughters in the U.S. today. As Rosa's visit to her childhood home in Miami demonstrated, it was her mother who prepared the meal, shopped for the food with a cousin and then spent hours in the kitchen. From Latino to Asian families, this dynamic is typical of many immigrant families. In Chicana families, for example, food preparation is a domain for women (Albarca 119-144), as it also is for Tejana women (Williams 113-126) and for many Asian women, such as Chinese (Liu and Lianlian 135-162), Indian (Beagan and

D'Sylva 210-222), Bengali (Zaman), and Vietnamese (Marquis and Shatenstein 77-82). The kitchen is indeed a singular place in immigrant households not only for nurturing family and for social gatherings but also for sharing knowledge and traditions (Hadjiyanni and Helle 97-116).

As women cook together and create extravagant traditional meals, they spend hours discussing family life; these lively discussions illustrate the value of meals as a social time and as a time for bonding (Meyers 13). In both author's families, our mothers' efforts to press food on the family not only shows how food serves as a bridge across generations of women (Meyers 105) but also shows immigrant mothers' pride in their cooking. The pride that these immigrant mothers take in their cooking reflects the reality that food may be the only common connection that they have left to their home culture and that without the food, the connection to their home culture may be forever cut (at least in their own minds). For many immigrant mothers, the community and bonding rewards of preparing and eating a meal justify their intense labour. Because a mother cooks as a means of identity and connection, cooking can contribute to her sense of self (Meyers 10).

The fact that women in both our families use traditional ethnic cuisine for celebrations and special occasions, but eat a more standard Americanized diet in their everyday lives, is indicative of a common phenomenon among immigrants: an acculturation to the mainstream culture, with the continuation of traditional cultural norms (Kalcik 38). The focus on foods from the home country at special occasions reaffirms ethnic identity (Ray 5; Zaman 25; Children's Health Watch) even as it grounds immigrants in their new home country.

HOW WE STUDIED THE FOOD PRACTICES OF
CARIBBEAN IMMIGRANT MOTHERS

We grounded this study in lived experience, utilizing qualitative ethnographic research with semi-structured interviews of four Caribbean immigrant mothers. Semi-structured interviews allow for the gathering of information about food practices that cannot be observed effectively by other means (Lindlof and Taylor 173).

This methodology made for richer data collection (especially given that this is a pilot study) and can give us insights into food practices from the perspectives of the immigrant women, leading us to understand "the social actor's experience and perspective" (Lindlof and Taylor 173) and to enhance "the representational richness and reflexivity of qualitative research" (Humphreys 840).

We used semi-structured interview techniques following Spradley's methods in *The Ethnographic Interview*. Spradley suggests that in the course of ethnographic interviewing the pattern of questions may vary according to the kind of responses provided by each informant. Ethnographic interviews should, however, begin with questions that seek general overviews of the events and activities under study, and then move to questions that deal with smaller aspects of the experience (Spradley 48-53).

Our interviews began with demographic questions related to the current age of each participant, age at immigration, and how long lived in the U.S. Interviewees were then asked the two main questions: "Please describe your food preparation on a typical day in your home country, from shopping to food preparation and eating" and "Please describe your food preparation on a typical day today, from shopping to food preparation and eating." The semi-structured interview included dialogue, and (where appro priate) clarification and expansion questions.

Four different Caribbean mothers—three from Puerto Rico and one from Santo Domingo—were interviewed, and their demo graphic information follows. (Interviewee names were changed to protect privacy; interviewees are referred to as Sofia, Camille, Valentina, and Esperanza.) Sofia, sixty-seven, is a twice-divorced woman who immigrated to the U.S. at the age of four and lives in a working-class neighbourhood in Miami, Florida. She has three children, twelve grandchildren, and five great-grandchil- dren. Camille, seventy, is a widow who immigrated to the U.S. at age of fifteen and lives in a middle-class neighbourhood in Hialeah, Florida. She lives with her eldest daughter, and she has three children and five grandchildren. Esperanza, sixty-seven, is a twice-married woman who immigrated to the U.S. in her mid-twenties and lives in a working-class neighbourhood in Miami, Florida. She has two sons and two grandchildren. Valentina, forty-seven, is a married woman who immigrated to the U.S. at age fourteen and lives in a working class neighbourhood in Paterson, New Jersey, with her husband, her four children and her one great-grandchild.

The four immigrant women discussed their food practices in their home country and the U.S. A few common themes about food emerged during the interviews. One primary theme reflected food collection and preparation. Each woman spoke to how food collection in the U.S. was a different experience than it had been in their home countries. Camille and Valentina were brought up on farms in the Caribbean. Sofia grew up in the mountains of Puerto Rico, not on a farm but on land that did grow much of the food that they ate. Esperanza grew up in an isolated small pueblo on the mountainous side of Puerto Rico. In the U.S., all four women lived at a distance from the origins of their food that they ate; they had to buy it from grocery stores and supermarkets, where naturally produced foods are difficult to find.

When the interviewees compared food in the islands to food in the U.S., they said that the locally produced food in their home countries was far healthier than the store-bought, non-local food in the U.S. Camille and Valentina believed that local fresh foods in their homeland were healthier than food bought at supermarkets in the U.S. The issue weighed heavily on them as both expressed nostalgia for the time when food was in their backyards and was grown without chemicals. They spoke about growing beans and vegetables, and having ready-access to milk, chickens, and eggs. For them, the *finca* (farm) was more than simply land; it was a place where large families and neighbours could be nurtured. All four interviewees mentioned that the food in the United States was overly processed and less healthy than the food produced in their home countries. Camille and Valentina both lamented the loss of the ability to grow their own foods and to share the experience of the land with their children. (Their concerns with healthy local foods resonate with us as we spend time trying to find locally grown vegetables, cage-free and organic eggs.) Pointing to a photo of her family, Sofia mentioned that they were skinnier in Puerto Rico. She noted that growing food from the land in Puerto Rico created a stronger ethic about both nurturing and consuming healthier food.

Today, she felt her family was less healthy: both her daughters had had weight-reduction surgeries. Esperanza reflected on the higher cost of food in the U.S. compared to that grown on the land in her home country, where many families had chickens, goats, and access to home-grown vegetables and fruits.

Another common theme was a sense of loss in the amount of cooking done in their daily lives. Although one of the women still cooked daily, and the others occasionally cooked for big family meals, in their daily lives, all four women generally ate less elaborately prepared meals (such as processed meals or easily microwavable dinners) or Americanized fast food. Esperanza did not eat what she'd cooked but instead ate health-conscious choices. Esperanza lived with her husband who was on disability benefits. She loved to cook elaborate traditional meals, but she noted that she herself never ate the traditional high-fat, high-starch Puerto Rican food, nor did she eat rice, red meat, crackers, or drink soda. Rather, she mostly ate *ensalada* (salads) and *un bote* (jar) *de garbanzo* beans. Esperanza struggled with issues of weight and had a family history of diabetes, and this was evident in her ambivalence towards food. Also, no longer having to cook for a large family meant that she could spend more time on faster, quicker meals. She only cooked elaborate meals when family members were in town. For Sofia, whose children were grown and were living farther away in Miami and Orlando (with one son in jail), mothering had taken a different course. She noted that she was estranged from her two daughters and was saddened by the reality that she no longer had anyone to cook for.

Sofia was a baker who had enjoyed baking traditional pastries for her family and the entire neighbourhood. But as tastes changed and people drifted away from the traditional labour-intensive and expensive foods, it was easier and cheaper for most people she knew to buy a sheet cake or a store-bought pastry. The loss of the role of neighbourhood baker left her saddened, and she now she spent most of her days watching TV and gardening. Sofia's loneliness was clear throughout the interview as she tried to share all that she knew about cooking with her interviewer whom she treated like a replacement daughter, and with whom she could share her cooking knowledge.

By contrast, Camille had relinquished much of the cooking in her household to her eldest daughter (with whom she lived). Meals were now smaller and more health-conscious. For bigger family events, however, Camille would often prepare more traditional meals. Occasionally, on Sundays, when their entire family got together, she would teach the traditional meals to her daughters and grandsons in the kitchen. Camille was unique among the interviewees as all her daughters lived in Miami, close to her. On the day of the interview, two of her three daughters were present. (We note that interviews with mothers and daughters could prove fruitful for future research, and we plan on extending this study to Latina mothers and daughters and to Indian-American immigrants.)

Unlike Sofia, Camille, and Esperanza (who were older and retired), Valentina cooked daily and spent more time cooking for her family than the other interviewees did. Valentina was the only interviewee who lived with her extended family, including her husband, two daughters, two sons, a granddaughter, and a son-in-law. The staples in her kitchen were rice, beans, and some fried meat (traditional Caribbean foods that all four participants mentioned repeatedly). Valentina noted that her mother-in-law had taught her to cook for her *esposo* (husband), which subtly suggested that her role as wife and mother would involve food.

Unusually, Valentina never indicated that she was preoccupied by food choices (as Sofia, Camille, and Esperanza were). It appears that since cooking for large families was no longer a priority, Sofia, Camille and Esperanza were more focused on eating and contrasting "healthy" eating with traditional, "less healthy" eating. In addition to showing how living without children affected eating choices, Sofia's, Camille's and Esperanza's views also shows the impact of age on attitudes towards traditional foods, as the interviewees started to struggle with issues like high cholesterol, diabetes, and weight gain.

All four interviewees repeatedly focused on health and on weight. For example, Valentina, who still had to cook for a large family, mentioned that genetics must be a factor because her children and grandchildren were skinnier than she was, although they all ate daily the same things that she cooked: *arroz moros, arroz con gandules,* and *platano frito,* foods seen in an idealized American diet as less than healthy because of their high starch and fat content. Esperanza mentioned high sugar as a factor in her food choices and constant dieting. Camille, who was a more recent immigrant and could not drive, noted that her food choices were affected by her husband's having to buy the food for the household and his desire for "real" (rice, beans, and some sort of fried meat) home-cooked food.

CONCLUSION

The voices and lived experiences of these four immigrant mothers in food practices within one immigrant community in the U.S. highlight the following themes: food nostalgia and identity, food as a way of mothering, and eating choices in new host country. What we learned from our interviews illuminates the place of food in the lives of Caribbean immigrants in the U.S. Food remains important for the reinforcement and nurturing of family, for the strengthening of community, and as a focus of celebrations. For all the interviewees, cooking traditional foods was inextricably linked with family. Food was also important in terms of ethnic identity. Here, traditional foods play a dual role: it is associated on the one hand with nostalgia for the home country and on the other with assimilation into the mainstream U.S. culture.

The issues important in the foodways of Caribbean-American immigrant women are common to many immigrant families, whether a Latina woman like Rosa (Albarca 119-144; Hadjiyanni and Helle 97-116; Williams 113-126) or an Asian woman like Pixy (Beagan and D'Sylva 210-222; Liu and Lianlian 135-162). Such a commonality of experience makes this study of relevance beyond the Caribbean community.

However, this study points to an issue significantly unique to the Caribbean community: the Caribbean diet. The everyday foods comprising this diet are high in starch and fat and significantly low in fresh fruits and vegetables. This can be seen in Sofia, Camille, Valentina and Esperanza's discussion of diets in their home countries and family celebrations in the U.S. In understanding the Caribbean diet, it's important to know that the traditional Caribbean diet was restricted by what was available on the islands, which was often limited. The diet relied on staples such as rice, beans, dried codfish (*bacalao*), and pork often prepared by frying. Although space prohibits us from discussing this diet in more detail, it is of note that Caribbean immigrants experience greater food conflicts as they are torn between nostalgic associations of traditional foods and healthy associations of the idealized American diet.

Finally, we note that although this is a preliminary study, it already, in many ways, raises several questions of broader interest, with a potential to illuminate the connections among the multiple influences of culture on immigrant mother-child food practices. Food practices of immigrant mothers assume ever greater importance given that children of immigrants are the fastest growing child population in the United States. (Children's Health Watch estimates that more than twenty percent of children under age six have immigrant parents.) This particular study has dealt with food practices of Caribbean immigrant mothers, but our results support (and are supported by) several other studies of immigrant food practices in other North American communities. We plan to continue our research and look forward to wider findings.

WORKS CITED

Albarca, Meredith M. "Los chilaquilas de mi'ama: The Language of Everyday Cooking." *Pilaf, Pozole and Pad Thai: American Women and Ethnic Food*. Ed. Sherrie A. Inness. Amherst, MA: University of Massachusetts Press, 2001. 119-144. Print.

Beagan, Brenda N. and Andrea D'Sylva. "Occupational meanings of Food Preparation for Goan Canadian women." *Journal of Occupational Science* 18.31 (2011): 210-222. Print.

Children's Health Watch. *Children of Immigrants. Healthy Beginnings Derailed by Food Insecurity. Children's Health Watch Policty Action Brief*. CHW, n.d. Web. 2 Nov. 2015.

Dillon, Frank R., Mario De La Rosa and Gladys E. Ibanez. "Acculturative Stress and Diminishing Family Cohesion among Recent Latino Immigrants." *Journal of Immigrant and Minority Health* 15.3 (2015): 484-491. Print.

Gerchow, Lauren, Barbara Tagliaferro, Alison Squires, Joey Nicholson, Stella M. Savarimuthu, Damara Gutnick, and Melanie Jay. "Latina Food Patterns in the United States: A Qualitative Metasynthesis." *Nursing Research* 63.3 (2014): 182-193. Print.

Hadjiyanni, Tasoulla and Kristin Helle. "Kitchens as Cultural Mediums – The Food Experiences of Mexican Immigrants in Minnesota." *Housing and Society Special Issue on Kitchens and Baths* 35.2 (2008): 97-116. Print.

Humphreys, Michael. "Getting Personal: Reflexivity and Autoethnographic Vignettes." *Qualitative Inquiry* 11.6 (2005): 840-860. Print.

Kalcik, Susan. "Ethnic Foodways in America: Symbol and the Performance of Identity." *Ethnic and Regional Foodways in the United States*. Eds. Linda Keller Brown and Kay Mussell. Knoxville, TN: University of Tennessee Press, 1984. 37-65. Print.

Lee, Helen M. "Second Generation Transnationalism." *Ties to the Homeland: Second Generation Transnationalism*. Ed. Helen M. Lee. Newcastle Upon Tyne: Cambridge Scholars Publishing, 2008. 1-32. Print.

Lindlof, Thomas R. and Bryan C. Taylor. "Asking, Listening, and Telling." *Qualitative Communication Research Methods*. Eds. Thomas R. Lindlof and Bryan C. Taylor. Thousand Oaks, CA: Sage, 2002. 170-208. Print.

Liu, Haiming and Lin Lianlian. "Food, Culinary Identity, and Transnational Culture: Chinese Restaurant Business in Southern California." *Journal of Asian American Studies* 12.2 (2009): 135-162. Print.

Meyers, Miriam. *A Bite of Mama's Plate: Mothers' and Daughters' Connections through Food*. Westport, CT: Bergin and Garvey, 2001. Print.

Ray, Krishnendu. *The Migrant's Table: Meals and Memories in Bengali-American Households*. Philadelphia, PA: Temple University Press, 2004. Print.

Rodriguez, Maripili and Yesi Morillo-Gual." Is Our Culture Killing Us." Proud to Be a Latina. New York City. 11 August 2014 2014. Lecture.

Spradley, James P. *The Ethnographic Interview*. New York: Harcourt, Brace, Jovanovich, 1979. Print.

Williams. Brett. "Why Migrant Women Feed Their Husbands

Tamales: Foodways as a Basis for a Revisionist View of Tejano Family Life." *Ethnic and Regional Foodways in the United States*. Eds Linda Keller Brown and Kay Mussell. Knoxville, TN: University of Tennessee Press, 1984. 113-126. Print.

Yeh, Ming-chin, Anahi Viladrich, Nancy Bruning, and Carol Roye. "Determinants of Latina Obesity in the United States: The Role of Selective Acculturation." *Journal of Transnational Nursing* 20.1 (2009): 105-115. Print.

Zaman, Tasmin. *Food, Identity and Symbolic Metaphors in the Bengali South Asian-Canadian Community.* Diss. University of Waterloo, 2010. Print.

17.
The Cooking Lesson

Identity and Spirituality in the Lives of Hindu Refugees in America

DOROTHY ABRAM

WOMEN, MOTHERS ESPECIALLY, ARE OFTEN ignored despite the strength and courage that they display during times of conflict and ethnic genocide. It is the mothers who sustain the family and maintain the community when their husbands, sons, and daughters are arrested, tortured, or made to disappear, and it is the mothers who protest for civil rights and equal treatment under the law. Without a choice and out of necessity, mothers shoulder the burden of the family's survival. In the dramatic monologue that follows this introduction, ritual and food are means of that sustenance. Their stories need to be told and heard. This is one such story.

The 2010 U.S. Senate Committee on Foreign Relations issued a report titled *Abandoned Upon Arrival: Implications for Refugees and Local Communities Burdened by a U.S. Resettlement System that Is Not Working.* This report specifically recommended that a new response is needed "to highlight and support innovative models of community support ... to make inter-ethnic encounters less intimidating for all participants." It recommended a "community engagement strategy for increasing public awareness of and interaction with refugees, in order to achieve greater community cohesion" (6).

This recommendation describes the work of the AWARE Alliance Refugee Theatre. The plays that we present, derived from the oral histories of refugees, affirm their experiences. Through the power of performance, their stories come to life for the communities in which they resettle. Theatre serves to connect refugees, students, and our extended community in a deepened understanding of the complexities, needs, and experiences of global exile and re-settlement. The dramatic monologue included in this collection on mothers and food is part of the story of a Bhutanese refugee woman living in Providence, RI, USA. It tells only one part of one story of the terror of ethnic cleansing that this Nepali-speaking Bhutanese family endured—and there are one hundred thousand more of these stories from Bhutan.

This dramatic monologue also speaks to the importance of under-standing the significant frameworks for survival that refugees bring with them. The following excerpt, titled "The Cooking Lesson", is part of my larger series of plays called *Circles of Sel Roti. An Unfolding of Plays on Identity and Spirituality in the Lives of Hindu Refugees in America.* In it, a Bhutanese refugee woman describes the plight of the disappearance and torture of her husband by the Bhutanese government during the ethnic cleansing. Both wife and husband relied on their Hindu religious beliefs to sustain them through and after this crisis of survival. For Chandra, the wife, it was her dedicated performance of a ritual for over five years that promised her the return of her husband. For her husband, it was his prayers to the Hindu god, Shiva, and his hope of return that enabled him to survive five years of imprisonment and torture for his protests for civil and human rights in Bhutan.

This dramatic monologue offers us a challenge: can we recognize and respond to the different cultural models of healing.

PLAY: THE COOKING LESSON

Character:
Chandra: wife and mother in the Acharya family, who are Ne-pali-Bhutanese refugees resettled in the United States.

Setting:
Chandra is giving cooking lessons on *sel roti* (Nepalese fried bread) to a group of Americans.

First, everyone wash your hands. Good. Now, write the recipe down as I prepare it for you to make next time. You need three kinds of flour: rice, wheat, and a kind of corn flour that here they call *sooji*. And a very large bowl. I don't remember the first time I made sel-roti, but you have this evening's cooking class to mark today's date for you. In Nepal, and as Nepali Bhutanese, we grow up with sel-roti. It's the scent and taste of joy and celebration, and also marks when we feel sadness, too. Sel-roti is always present at all our feasts—at marriage and death, and everything in between— every parting and every reunion features sel-roti.

You'll see when we squeeze the batter into the hot mustard oil that we make sure that we overlap the ends of the batter in the oil. That's important to us Nepalese. It means that ends in our lives will overlap with their beginnings and so promises us that we will meet again. Sel-rotis signal the hope of return and reunion. When we eat sel-roti together, we know that we will meet again. Perhaps we'll meet again at another cooking class after tonight, too! Ha.

In the refugee camps, we didn't have cooking classes. We just figured out how to cook our monthly allotment of rice, and everything else too, through eighteen years—yes, eighteen years in the refugee camps. Bhutan would not allow us to return to our homes and treated us as if we were criminals. They considered us terrorists for wanting civil rights for us Hindus of the south. It didn't make sense. Pardon? What's that? How many calories? We never count calories, so I wouldn't know. Yes, sel-roti means "fried-bread." No, it's not too fattening! I told you: we eat them all the time....

Before I left for America, they told me that I'd gain a lot of weight after I come here and that I should sew some really huge cholis—you know, the bra part of the sari? The six-yard sari fabric is, obviously, expandable. How big? I asked them. This big? This bigger? This biggest—wow?! You could fit our entire community in that, and a couple of water buffalos, too! I don't know why it didn't happen to me, why I didn't get fat, too. I ate Nepalese food there; I eat Nepalese food here. But my littlest boys! They like french fries better than sel-rotis! Can you even imagine such a thing? Yes, we eat potatoes, but rice is our food, our blessing. Yes, rice.

Speaking of blessing.... Did you know that the first thing Buddha did when he became the Buddha was to outlaw the caste system in

Buddhism? Ha! Guess what? The first thing this supposed Buddhist government did in Bhutan was to make sure that we Hindus were lower than the untouchables—to curse us and exile us! If you act as if you have a caste system, it doesn't matter if you actually call it caste or not. That's what I think.

Oh my, have I lost my focus with our sel-roti lesson? Goodness, let's see. Now, blend the flours in the bowl, and you can add a touch of baking powder just to give the bread a nice puffiness, though the most accomplished cooks claim that they don't need baking powder to get that effect. Ha! Even I add the baking powder, and no one makes better sel-roti than I do. Now, slowly add the milk—it's my secret, the milk, that is, so that the rings don't absorb too much oil. No, we won't use a spoon, no mixer either! We use our hands, the best utensil there is. This way, you feel the texture of the batter. You sense the lumps that try to run by and you catch them between your fingers, and—press! Ahh, the batter feels silky and smooth. That is when you are done. With mixing the batter, that is.

Let's heat the mustard oil—yes, mustard! You can use vegetable, but mustard is better. Heat the oil in a large frying pan. Hot enough so a speck of batter thrown into the depths of the oil then swims beautifully in a golden bath with bubbles as it rises to the surface. That's how hot it should be. Yes, you smell it? The aroma of mustard oil is quite strong. It took me a long time to be able to smell it again after ... yes, after that ... but now I can. What? What did you ask? Why I reacted to the scent of mustard oil? No, it wasn't an allergy. We don't have allergies in Nepal. When we first arrived in the United States, my daughter came home from school and asked if she could have an allergy like the other children in her class. I didn't know what an allergy was, but I promised her one, if we could afford it, that is, for the holiday. Then I found out. Allergies. What a concept! To resist food as if it were an enemy. In Nepal, we use foods for medicines. We use them to cure sickness, not to cause it. Sometimes it's hard to understand the ways here.

Okay, the batter is ready and the oil is hot. Oh, yes, someone go outside and find a branch, that is, a stick about this long, remove the leaves, and whittle it to a point. Why are you all standing there?

Someone has to do it. Well, yes, I suppose we could use tongs, but they don't work as well as a sharpened stick. Why do you have to buy everything when it's so easy to make it yourself? I don't understand, really. Ok, now we need a plate to put them on. That's it. Grab a handful of batter. Just a palm full, it's the exact amount. Like this. Squeeze it into the oil—be careful, it's very hot—into a circle with overlapping ends. That's very important; they must overlap. You see? Easy! Now, you try. Be careful. Yes, well, that's not quite a circle, but that's ok. Watch again. Like this. Hmm, um, well ... no, like this ... Let me show you. Not so hard, yes? No, that's not it. That's more like a ziggle. Oh, ziggle is not a word? But, you just made one. Let me show you again. Like this. I have done it for so long and so often that it seems simple, but I suppose it does take some practice. I make 108 sel-rotis every year for just one holiday alone. Swasthani. And then there's Shivatri, and Tihar and ... so many holidays in Hinduism. And for the children, of course. Yes, I have four boys. Well, it was when I had just given birth to my twins, my two youngest boys. Yes, Lok and Laksmi. You met them when you came? Good boys, identical twins. We joke now that they are the family's bad luck. Oh, yes, just a joke, though very shortly after they were born, just a few days later, the police took my husband away and jailed him for his protests for civil rights. Such a difficult time. You see, it's not like here where you have rights and a legal system to rely on. Once he disappeared into the Bhutanese jail system, I couldn't find him again. It was a good thing that I didn't know he was being tortured then, or I don't think I could have survived the heartache. It was hard enough, as it was, having the four boys to care for. I cried every night. Is that any way to bring up children?

The only thing that I could really do to effect the situation and to bring my beloved Laksman home again was to beg the Goddess to bestow this boon. You need more oil in the pan ... Yes, that's enough.... What was I saying? Ah, yes, Swasthani. That's the holiday that I mentioned before. You never heard of it? It comes every year, and for a month, we—mostly women, that is—fast, and read the Swasthani scripture, and bathe in sacred waters. When the Goddess sees such devotion and dedication, she may grant us our prayer. And that's what I did, every year, for five years. Part of this ritual is to make 108 sel-rotis. I mixed and fried and mixed and fried until I filled the whole house with the sweet scent of sel-rotis cooking in pungent mustard oil. No, we don't have glazed sel-rotis. I said sweet because sel-rotis are such sweet pleasure for us.

Yes, as I was saying, at the fifth year, when I was finally on the final eight of the 108, the most unexpected—well, unexpected, but anticipated, too—thing happened. I had just lifted the 108th sel-roti from the pan when the door opened and in walked Laksman. Well, in came Laksman carried by his two brothers. He was so weak. I placed eight sel-rotis on a platter, as the ritual requires, and walked over to Laksman as if he hadn't even been absent for the past five years!—and offered him the fresh, hot, fragrant sel-rotis. You see, the wife must offer 8 of the 108 sel-rotis to her husband, that's the ritual. Why? I don't know why. We don't ask those questions, we just do it, experience it. That's how you truly understand. Look how good you made that sel-roti! Try again. You see? Once you experience it, you understand and the questions are answered without even being asked. So, as I was saying.... Somehow, Laksman, so frail and weak that he could not even stand on his own, managed to smile at me before he collapsed on the chair. Or was it because of the scent of sel-rotis? You see, the Goddess had finally granted my request. Laksman had returned because I had performed Swasthani with devotion for five years.

What do you mean "why five years"? Prayers aren't just answered for nothing in Hinduism, just because you want it. What do you call that here? I know you have a word for it ... is it, instant coffee? No ... um, instant ticket? No, not that either ... I know! Instant gratification! You want it, you get it. So, why do you need devotion or gods? It's not like at the supermarket here where if you have the right coupon, everything is free and fast. I even saw on television that a woman had so many coupons that the store paid her real money to take away a wagon full of groceries. Why did she need so much shampoo when she had four boys just like me, and they all had shaved heads? But, it was free so she was so happy, especially because her neighbours were so jealous, and she got to be on TV and she became a star, a big famous person, for cutting out coupons and winning all that shampoo—shampoos that did the most amazing things, miracles even. Like it made her hair sing like a loud radio, that was the shampoo with volume. Look, we're almost done with the sel-rotis. Oh, my, I forgot again what I was telling you....

Oh, yes, about how the goddess Swasthani answered my prayer that Laksman returned to me from prison. Why are you shaking your head? And you, you're rolling your eyes? You don't believe me? Of course, she did. You don't think so? I have the evidence. He returned during the festival of Swasthani, just in time to be given the husband's portion of the sel-rotis. That proves it. You still shake your head? What evidence do you have that his return didn't happened through the intervention of the gods? Sel-roti ... returns ... Swasthani ... the beginning meets the end. And there he was, finally, after so many years. My prayers were finally answered.

What? You've already started eating the sel-rotis? Oh, my. Why? No, it's not exactly wrong. It's just that we usually take the first pieces, the best pieces, and offer them to our god. No, it's not a sacrifice. Well, at least not a sacrifice as you may mean with knives and blood and gore and things like that. Actually, it sort of is a sacrifice, but it's an offering. Yes, we believe that our god.... What? Where is he? In the family shrine upstairs, of course. What did you say? Like room service? I don't understand. What is service to a room? No, we are serving our god. What do you mean "Does he eat the sel-rotis?" Why do you laugh? Of course, he does, what else? Oh, my, that really isn't the point, is it? Okay, let me think for a moment how to explain this. You see, we practise giving the best breads, the first sel-rotis, away, to our god, Shiva. That is a holy act. It shows that we can control our desires and greed for a greater good. What greater good, you ask? It demonstrates our selflessness. Well, yes, of course, we eat it later. No, that's not god's room service—whatever that means! You see, the food has changed in the meantime by being offered to our god. It becomes what we call *prasad*, blessed food. It tastes divine and delicious! We collect the entire prasad and then divide it into equal parts so that everyone has a portion to enjoy—that's justice for all! It's sort of like when you say grace before a meal. Only then, that's all words and no actions that demonstrate your faith. No, I'm not judging you. In Hinduism, we believe that everyone has their own path to follow in life. Really. Well, think of it this way. Life is like a sel-roti. It's true! All parts of a sel-roti are made of the same batter and they circle around the same center, even if they are eaten by different people. Get it? Sel-roti is the symbol and the substance of life itself!

Now, help yourself to this platter of sel-rotis. Oh, my, I lose my focus so easily! And, we have so much more to cook together.... Next, we will make the hot chilli pepper pickles that go so well with Himalayan food. They're hot! Though we Nepalis don't think so. We like hot spicy food. It keeps us warm in the Himalayas. A question? Do we use food processors? Oh, yes, of course, and we'll use a food processor today, too. In Nepal we call it differently. We call it ... how do you say? Oh, yes, we call it a mortar and pestle. It does everything and fast too! Of course, if you don't have a mortar and pestle, you can always use a large, round, smooth stone that you can find on a walk outside. Obviously, you must be sure to wash and dry it first. When you find the correct grinding stone for your hand and for your uses, well, cooking is such a delight!

Now, let's start chopping the chillies. I like the little green ones, they're the hottest. Also, did I mention that I'll be moving soon? Ah, yes, maybe there will be more hope for us for jobs in Ohio where we have some relatives.... Our mother, our children's grandmother, wants to be close to the relatives, she has a brother there, and to have our entire family all together, all around her. Keep chopping, but don't touch your eyes! Yes, we do use knives. Well, if she wants this, we have to make it happen. She's the grandmother of the family, after all. A home, put her in a home? What do you mean? She has a home with us. In a home without her family, you say? What kind of home is that? I don't understand, but that's okay. We do things differently. The oldest is the wisest in our culture. When you reach that age, you've earned honour and respect, and the care of the rest of the family. Just as we will be cared for in our old age by our children. Oh my, does that thought make you all feel sad? Yes, I know things are done differently here. But not to worry! We ate sel-rotis together, so I'm sure that we'll meet again!

WORK CITED

Abram, Dorothy. *Circles of Sel Roti: An Unfolding of Plays on Identity and Spirituality in the Lives of Hindu Refugees in America*. Unpublished manuscript, 2012. Print.

United States. Senate. *Abandoned Upon Arrival: Implications for Refugees and Local Communities Burdened By A U.S. Resettlement System That Is Not Working*. 111th Congress, 2nd Session, July 21 2010. Washington: United States Government Printing Office, 2010.

Contributor Biographies

Dorothy Abram is a playwright and professor in the Social Sciences Department of Johnson & Wales University in Providence, Rhode Island. She is co-convener of the United Nations Subcommittee on Refugees, Immigrants, and Mental Health.

Lorin Basden Arnold is a professor of Communication Studies and dean of the College of Communication and Creative Arts at Rowan University. She completed her PhD at Purdue University, with a focus on interpersonal communication and gender. As a family communication and gender scholar, her research interrogates issues at the intersection of family beliefs/roles/expectations and gender beliefs/roles/expectations, and proceeds from a belief that understanding the parental experience is vital. She is a mother of six, a spouse, and a vegan.

Conrad Brunström is lecturer in English at Maynooth University in Ireland. An eighteenth-century literature specialist, he has published two monographs on the poetry of William Cowper (2004) and the oratory of Thomas Sheridan (2011). He has published and presented papers internationally on topics as diverse as religious literature, poetic form, theatre history, political rhetoric, and Queer Studies. He is currently researching Irish and Canadian nationalisms and the role of speechmaking in the formation of a sense of collective political identity.

Tanya M. Cassidy is a Canadian sociologist who received her doctorate from the University of Chicago. Recently, she won a competitive EU Horizon 2020 Marie Sklodowska Curie Fellowship housed at the University of Central Lancashire (UCLan). She continues to be an affiliated researcher in the Department of Anthropology at the Maynooth University (Ireland), where she held her Cochrane Fellowship, as well as an adjunct professor with the Department of Sociology, Anthropology, Criminology at the University of Windsor, Ontario (Canada).

Erica Cavanagh is an associate professor in the Department of English at James Madison University in Harrisonburg, Virginia, where she is spearheading efforts to establish a Food Studies minor. She holds a master's of Humanities from the University of Chicago and an MFA in nonfiction writing from the University of Iowa. Her essays have appeared in the *Missouri Review, Bellevue Literary Review, North American Review, Gastronomica,* and elsewhere.

Grace M. Cho is associate professor in the Department of Sociology and Anthropology at the College of Staten Island – City University of New York. She is author of *Haunting the Korean Diaspora: Shame, Secrecy and the Forgotten War* (University of Minnesota Press, 2008) and is currently working on a food memoir. Her memoir work has appeared in *Gastronomica, Contexts,* and *Qualitative Inquiry.*

Sharmila Pixy Ferris (PhD, Pennsylvania State University) is professor in the Department of Communication at William Paterson University in Wayne, New Jersey. She is coordinator of the Race and Gender Project, and for several years served as director of the Center for Teaching Excellence. Sharmila Pixy is an Indian-American woman whose research brings an interdisciplinary focus to computer-mediated communication, in which area she has published several books and many articles.

Sarah N. Gatson is associate professor at the Department of Sociology at Texas A&M University. She earned her MA and PhD in Sociology at Northwestern University. Her work focuses on identity, community, and citizenship, using a cultural, socio-legal, and intersectional lens. Her current project is grounded in service-learning and collaborative ethnographic research focused on community food security.

Thomas Guignard is an engineer turned librarian, currently project manager at the Ontario Colleges Library Service. He holds a MSc in Electrical Engineering from ETH Zurich and a PhD in Acoustics from EPFL (Switzerland), and he is working towards an MLS from Aberystwyth University (Wales). In his free time, he volunteers as a computer programming instructor at Software Carpentry workshops for academics. A maker and photographer, he enjoys cooking with his daughter and making things out of love, light, and cardboard.

Wendy Jones Nakanishi is professor of language and culture at Shikoku Gakuin University in Japan. She got her BA in English at Indiana University, her MA at Lancaster University (England), and PhD at Edinburgh University (Scotland) in 18th-century English studies. She has published widely in her academic field of English and Japanese literature from the 18th to the 21st century and, in recent years, she has begun writing creative nonfiction pieces about her life in Japan as an academic, the wife of a Japanese farmer, and the mother of three sons.

Joyce Mandell received her doctorate in sociology from Boston College in 2008. She served as a visiting assistant professor in Urban Studies and the director of the Center for Service Learning and Civic Engagement at Worcester State University in Massachusetts. She has written extensively in the area of service learning, community development, and community development corporations. In 2012, she left her position to care for her daughter who was diagnosed with celiac disease. Currently she is writing a memoir entitled, *Healing Hava: A Mother's Story of Love, Food, and Celiac Disease.*

B. Lee Murray is an associate professor at the College of Nursing, University of Saskatchewan. She is also a clinical nurse specialist in adolescent mental health. Her research project promotes healthy sexuality and the prevention of sexual abuse of adolescents with developmental disabilities. She also has a great interest and curiosity regarding mothering. To satisfy this curiosity, she uses autoethnography as a methodology to explore the normative discourse of mothering in the context of her own experiences as a mom and grandma.

Kari O'Driscoll is a mother of two and a writer living in the Seattle area. She studied medical ethics at Pacific University and writes about parenting and social justice on her blog and for various publications. She is also working to bring social-emotional learning to teens and their families through The SELF Project (www.theselfproject.com).

Dominique O'Neill was born and raised in France. She holds an MA in French Literature from the University of Toronto, and taught French at Glendon College (York University), where she also coordinated its Writing Workshop. She has since joined the York University Writing Department as an associate lecturer. Her passions are individual tutoring at the Writing Centre, the History of the Book, a course she offers to fourth year (book stream) Professional Writing students, and of course her family.

Florence Pasche Guignard completed her PhD in the study of religions at the University of Lausanne (Switzerland). In 2012, she joined the Department for the Study of Religion at the University of Toronto to complete her postdoctoral research project, funded by the Swiss National Science Foundation and entitled "Natural Parenting in the Digital Age. At the Confluence of Mothering, Religion, Environmentalism, and Technology." Her research engages issues at the intersection of religion, ritual, gender, embodiment, and material culture and integrates approaches from motherhood studies and media studies.

Christin L. Seher is a PhD candidate in Higher Education Administration at Kent State University and an instructor in the School of Nutrition and Dietetics at the University of Akron. She is interested in initiating critical conversations in the nutrition-dietetics profession around curriculum and professionalization practices, practice-policy, and cultural competence-diversity. She lives near Cleveland, Ohio, with her partner and son.

Robin Silbergleid is the author of the memoir *Texas Girl* (Demeter Press, 2014) and the collection of poems *The Baby Book* (CavanKerry Press, 2015). She is associate professor of English and director of Creative Writing at Michigan State University.

Rosa Soto (PhD, University of Florida) is an associate professor in the Department of English and director of the Latin American and Latino Studies Program at William Paterson University in Wayne, New Jersey. Rosa is a Puerto Rican woman, born in Miami, Florida, whose expertise is in Latino literature and American literature, with specialties in gender and popular culture. She is a board member of the New Jersey Council for the Humanities.

Meredith Stephens is on the faculty in the Department of Comparative Cultures at the Institute of Socio-Arts and Sciences at Tokushima University. She first studied Japanese and Linguistics at the University of Adelaide and then pursued a degree in Applied Linguistics at Macquarie University. Her research includes English language pedagogy in Japan and cross-cultural experiences of English speakers in Japan.

Emily Weiskopf-Ball is a PhD candidate in Laurentian University's Human Studies program. She also teaches English at École secondaire catholique Algonquin in North Bay, Ontario. Her research interests focus of traditional foodways, specifically French-Canadian foods. Her recent work studies the impact that gender and instructional methods have on maintaining traditional foodways. Inspired by her own mother, she strives to pass on the welcoming and inclusive kitchen culture that she grew up with to her own two daughters.